The United States Patent and Trademark Office's

Guide for Preparation of Patent Drawings

With a Practitioner's Comments on
Drawings for Electronic Filing
and
Drawings for Design Patent Applications
by Carl Oppedahl
of Oppedahl Patent Law Firm LLC

Penaya Publishing
www.penaya.com
Westminster, Colorado

ISBN 978-0984408436
Library of Congress control number 2012906908

Penaya Publishing
www.penaya.com

Introduction

Patent examiners and other personnel of the United States Patent and Trademark Office (USPTO) take their guidance for nearly all of their work from the United States Code, from the Code of Federal Regulations, and from the Manual of Patent Examining Procedure. But in the particular area of patent drawings, they take their guidance from a little-known work, now out of print at the Government Printing Office, called the *Guide for Preparation of Patent Drawings*. That *Guide* is reproduced here, along with a *Practitioner's Comment on Drawings for Electronic Filing* and a *Practitioner's Comment on Drawings for Design Patent Applications*.

Why is there a June 2002 edition of the *Guide for Preparation of Patent Drawings*? There are two reasons for the June 2002 edition of the *Guide*, namely a significant change in USPTO's internal processing of drawings that happened in 2002, and the advent of electronic filing of patent applications.

The change in internal processing of drawings. A patent application filed in the USPTO as the national phase from an international (Patent Cooperation Treaty) patent application is handled first by the part of PCT Operations that carries out national-phase processing (also known as DO/EO/US) and is later released to the Examining Corps for examination by a patent examiner as to patentability.

Any other patent application filed in the USPTO is handled first by the Office of Patent Application Processing (OPAP), formerly known as the Office of Initial Patent Examination (OIPE), and is later released to the Examining Corps for examination by a patent examiner as to patentability.

Before 2001, the first publication of any US patent application came at such time as the patent was issued. This meant that for a given patent application, any close scrutiny of the patent drawings usually happened for the first time during examination by the patent examiner assigned to the application. Stated differently, if a defect in a patent drawing was found, it was generally found by the patent examiner during the examination for patentability.

The American Inventor's Protection Act of 1999, however, directed the

USPTO to publish most patent applications about eighteen months after filing, and earlier in the case of an application claiming the domestic benefit of a previous US application or claiming the priority of a previous foreign application.

Such so-called "pre-grant publication", taking place long before issuance of a patent, would generally happen well before such time as the patent application had been taken up by a patent examiner. This meant that someone other than the patent examiner would have to review newly filed patent drawings to determine whether they were suitable for pre-grant publication. This task fell to the OIPE (now OPAP) and to DO/EO/US. This change in the internal processing led to a need to train OIPE and DO/EO/US personnel so that defects in patent drawings in an application could be detected soon after filing and well before the pre-grant publication of the application. This is one of the reasons for the 2002 edition of the *Guide*.

The advent of electronic filing of patent applications. For the first 180 or so years of the US patent system, patent drawings were required by the USPTO to be hand-drawn in India ink on Bristol board (a kind of stiff white cardboard). In the 1980's there was a gradual shift toward drawings which had been photocopied or laser-printed onto plain paper. All such drawings were required to be physically delivered to the USPTO. (Fax filing was not permitted and there was no e-filing system.)

With the advent of pre-grant publication, USPTO launched a system for electronic filing of patent applications. The e-filing system accepted image files for the patent drawings, including images prepared by computer rather than by a human draftsperson. At about the same time, USPTO migrated from the use of paper files to a system of electronic files within the USPTO. These changes meant that USPTO personnel would be reviewing newly filed patent drawings on computer screens rather than by inspection of physical paper drawings. This, too, was a reason for the 2002 edition of the *Guide*.

The reason for this book. When USPTO prepared the 2002 *Guide*, which was a revision of the previous version published in October 1993, it made the *Guide* available for purchase by applicants and practitioners from the Superintendent of Documents at the U.S. Government Printing Office (GPO). Later, however, the GPO allowed the *Guide* to go out of print. This put applicants and practitioners in a difficult situation – the *Guide* was (and continues to this day) to be the authoritative reference for examination of patent drawings, and yet applicants and practitioners could not conveniently obtain copies of the *Guide*.

Fortunately there is no copyright impediment to the reproduction of the *Guide* in this book, because the *Guide* is a work of the United States government, and thus is not protected by copyright (*see* 17 USC § 105).

Practitioner's Comments. The *Guide* is an essential resource for anyone who is preparing drawings for filing in the USPTO, since it allows one to know what USPTO personnel will be looking for when they review the applicant's filed drawings. But there are important things that applicants need to know about patent drawings, that are not mentioned in the *Guide*. For this reason, two brief "practitioner's comments" follow, which are intended to communicate some of these things.

It is hoped that this book will be helpful to applicants and to practitioners in the US and around the world, as they prepare drawings for filing in the US Patent and Trademark Office.

Carl Oppedahl
Oppedahl Patent Law Firm LLC
www.oppedahl.com

A Practitioner's Comment on Drawings for Electronic Filing

The *Guide for Preparation of Patent Drawings* is prepared primarily as an instructional document for USPTO personnel. Its authors were not patent applicants or practitioners, and were not writing from such a perspective. As such, the *Guide* does not say very much about what the patent applicant must do in the preparation of image files for e-filing, so as to achieve satisfactory results.

As one example, the *Guide* says nothing about the need to avoid the use of gray scale in drawings.

Here is a patent drawing as originally prepared by the inventor. The USPTO e-filing system permits the filer to "preview" a drawing prior to submission of the patent application to the USPTO, and this is exactly how the drawing appeared in the preview screen. This is what was e-filed with the USPTO.	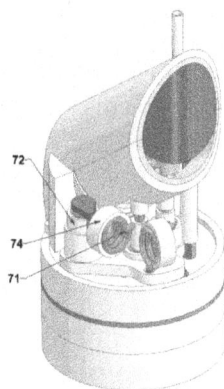
This is how USPTO published the image as Figure 3 in the pre-grant publication. Note the cross-hatching artifacts introduced by USPTO's conversion of the original image files into the internal format used by USPTO in its electronic file. Note that contrast between adjacent areas of shading has been badly degraded.	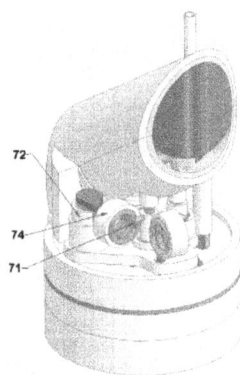

This is how USPTO published the image on the front page of the pre-grant publication. Note the even more extreme cross-hatching artifacts on a much coarser scale.

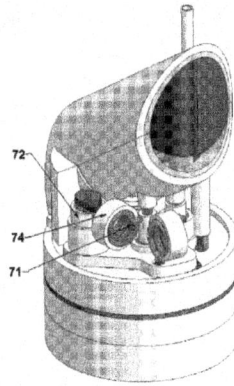

From this example one may see how a perfectly clear image, as e-filed, can be degraded, sometimes severely, by the USPTO's internal systems.

To avoid these problems, the applicant should avoid the use of any gray scale. One way to describe this is that the image must have a "color depth" of two. Stated differently, each pixel of the image must be either pure black or pure white.

It might be thought that such shading could be communicated by means of "half-toning", as used in comic strips and newspapers. The problem, however, is that USPTO will often rescale a drawing, making it larger or (more often) smaller to fit the page layout in USPTO's publication process. The rescaling often degrades the half-toning, sometimes almost to the point where an image is unrecognizable.

The applicant must, therefore, prepare drawings which will survive the image conversions and rescaling that happen within USPTO. So far as shading is concerned, the safest course is to use "spaced lines" or "stippling" as shown in the *Guide* at page 28 and at Examples 16 and 17 (pages A4-25 and A4-37).

As another example, the *Guide* says nothing about the need to avoid the use of lines that are only one pixel wide. A real-life example will illustrate this.

Here is the image as it was originally filed with the USPTO. In the "preview" screen prior to submission of the patent application by the applicant, the image looked exactly like this.

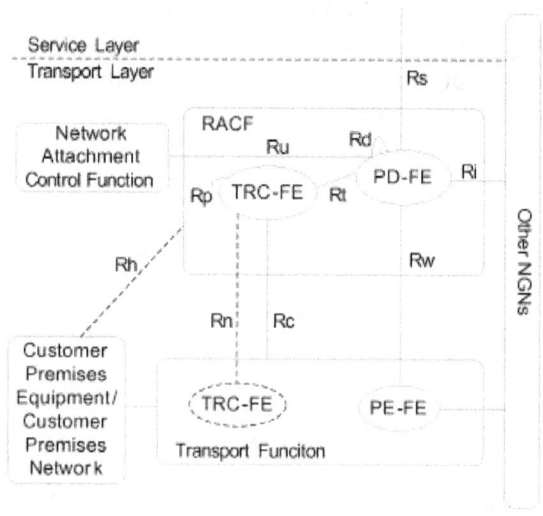

Here is the image as published by USPTO in the pre-grant publication. USPTO re-sized the image by discarding about every tenth column of pixels. The result is that some vertical lines were completely lost in USPTO's re-sizing process.

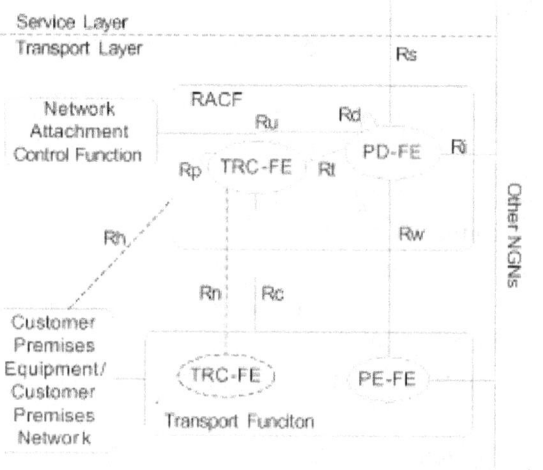

In this particular case the re-sizing was horizontal, and so the lost lines were vertical lines. But as a general matter, any feature that is only one pixel wide can get lost in USPTO's resizing process.

To avoid this problem, the applicant should ensure that any line or feature is at least two pixels in both horizontal and vertical extent.

The use of landscape orientation. If the filer files a drawing in landscape orientation instead of portrait orientation, one might be forgiven for assuming that USPTO would simply rotate the sheet to portrait orientation.

This is not, however, what USPTO does with such a sheet. USPTO's e-filing system instead "squeezes" the drawing in one dimension, so that (for example) the eleven-inch dimension is squeezed down to eight and a half inches. The resulting image is often nearly unrecognizable. The aspect ratio changes, so that for example what was once a circle becomes an ellipse, and what was once a square becomes a rectangle.

To avoid this problem, each page of the e-filed drawings must be in portrait orientation. If necessary, images may be rotated using an image editor such as Irfanview.

The unhelpfulness of the "preview" process in USPTO's e-filing system. In each of the examples just given, the "preview" process in the e-filing system showed the image just as it was prepared by the applicant. The previewed image gave no hint or suggestion of the degradations that would follow later in USPTO's publication process. From this it is evident that one cannot trust the "preview" process to determine whether an image will achieve good results in the USPTO pre-grant publication or in the issued patent.

The only real value of the "preview" process in USPTO's e-filing system is to permit the filer to detect the inadvertent uploading of a completely wrong image file, such as a set of figures for a completely different patent application.

Practitioner review of images prior to e-filing. If the person preparing the image is familiar with the points raised in this book, he or she may sidestep problems by avoiding the use of gray scale, and avoiding the use of too-thin lines. But very often the practitioner faces the situation where drawings have been prepared by the inventor, and only the inventor knows just how the drawings were prepared. This raises the question how the practitioner may anticipate image problems and, hopefully, correct such problems prior to filing.

A first level of review is a simple visual inspection. The practitioner can see gray scale, or the use of

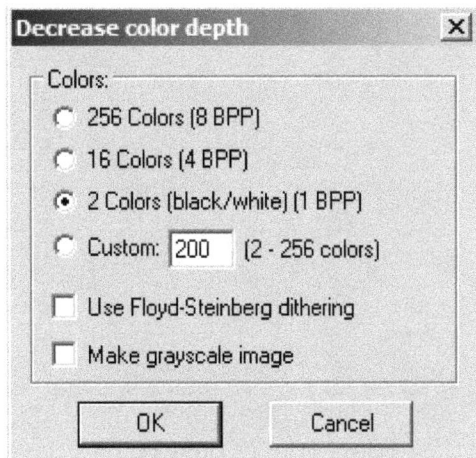

color, or the use of too-thin lines, and can refer the images back to the inventor for revision.

A second level of review is to carry out tests upon an image. Open the image in an image editor, such as Irfanview, and reduce the color depth to two colors, as shown in this screen shot. If the image degrades appreciably, then it should probably be revised prior to filing.

Practitioner review of images after e-filing. Another important step is to review drawing images *after* the patent application has been e-filed. This may be done in Private PAIR (USPTO's system that allows applicants to see what is in USPTO's files). This review should be done immediately after the patent application has been filed, and well before midnight Eastern Time. This permits plenty of time to e-file additional drawings if necessary, or in extreme cases to refile the entirety of the patent application, without loss of a filing date.

Joining the EFS-Web-L listserv. Oppedahl Patent Law Firm LLC sponsors a listserv for users of the USPTO patent e-filing system. Many e-filing issues are discussed there, including problems with patent drawings. Practitioners should join the listserv so as to keep abreast of problems and possible solutions to the problems. Instructions for joining the listserv may be seen at http://www.oppedahl.com/listserves .

Carl Oppedahl
Oppedahl Patent Law Firm LLC
www.oppedahl.com

A Practitioner's Comment on
Drawings for Design Patent Applications

Any time that an applicant files a patent application in the USPTO, there is a risk that USPTO will later find some real or perceived defect in a drawing of that patent application, and will require that a replacement drawing be filed. What exactly are the consequences if a patent drawing is deemed to be defective?

In a utility patent application, most often the consequence of a defective drawing is merely the expense associated with the preparation and filing of a replacement drawing.

In a design patent application, however, the consequence of a defective drawing can be, and often is, the loss of a filing date. The loss of a filing date can lead to a complete loss of all substantive patent rights in the US because of a statutory bar, or at the least can lead to a loss of a priority claim under Article 4 of the Paris Convention. The problem, of course, is that when a replacement drawing is filed in a design patent application, the Examiner is likely to be of the view that the replacement drawing adds "new matter" to the patent application.

From this it will be appreciated that it is extremely important to take whatever steps are necessary to prepare satisfactory drawings *prior to filing day*. Waiting until *after* filing day to prepare satisfactory design drawings is an invitation to disaster.

Choosing when to have formal design drawings prepared. USPTO patent filing procedures do permit filing a design application with informal drawings, in which case the applicant is invited to file formal drawings at a later time. When there is little or no time available for filing a US design application, one may be forced by circumstance to file using informal drawings such as the original JPG drawings that were filed in a priority application. This approach is, however, almost certain to lead to great expense and uncertainty when the formal drawings are filed. The USPTO will often find real or imagined flaws in the formal drawings due to supposed introduction of "new matter" in the formal drawings, or due to non-identical content in the informal and formal drawings.

The best practice is that formal drawings be prepared *prior to* the filing of the US design application, and that the formal drawings be included in the design application from the beginning. These drawings must be *line drawings*, free from any gray scale or use of color. The drawings must provide a plurality of views including enough plan views to show everything about the article of manufacture that the applicant seeks to claim. It is desirable to provide at least one perspective view. The drawings must be labeled with figure numbers, and the drawing sheets should have sheet numbers.

Choosing whether to use a patent draftsperson. Sometimes an applicant will prefer to prepare his or her own drawings rather than making use of the services of a patent draftsperson, out of a desire to avoid the expense of the draftsperson's services. Such an approach usually ends up costing more money than if the draftsperson had been retained at the outset.

Filings claiming priority from non-US filings. In the experience of Oppedahl Patent Law Firm LLC, the single thing that causes the most frustration and undesired expense in a US design application, when it claims priority from a previous non-US application, is the attempt to use non-US drawings. Many non-US patent offices will accept a wide range of types of drawings, including gray scale and photographs. Such drawings, however, are almost certain to be rejected by USPTO. The only drawings which USPTO will accept are pure black and white line drawings. In the argot of image editors, such drawings "have a color depth" of two, meaning that each pixel is either pure black or pure white, and is no other color. If the image file is a JPG file, then it is almost surely not a good format for a US design filing.

Here are some examples of drawings from actual registered Community designs which, if identically filed as US design drawings, would almost certainly be rejected by the USPTO.

The USPTO's reasons for rejecting non-US drawings might include the use of color or the use of gray scale.

Picking a patent draftsperson. It is a best practice to make use of the services of a professional patent draftsperson having substantial experience with US design drawings, for the preparation of drawings for US design applications. Some patent draftspersons do only utility drawings and lack experience with design drawings.

Broken lines. Broken lines may be employed to indicate either environmental matter which is desirable for understanding but not part of

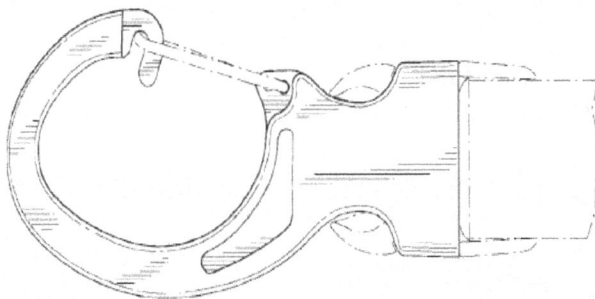

the claimed design, or elements of the article of manufacture that are not part of the claimed design. An issued US design patent employing such broken lines has a greater claim scope than one that does not. The thoughtful applicant will thus consider whether broken lines should be used in the drawings. Here is a drawing of a side-squeeze buckle showing the use of broken lines.

Providing views from all sides. USPTO examiners in design patent applications are trained that they should check carefully to make sure that all sides of the article of manufacture are depicted. If any side of the article is not shown in a drawing, the examiner is likely to object to the drawing and may take the position that the application as filed is not "enabling" under 35 USC § 112.

In some cases, due to symmetry in the article of manufacture, it may happen that one side of the article is identical in appearance to another side of the article, or is an exact mirror image thereof. In such a case the applicant can omit one of the two views, but only if text is provided in the application as filed communicating this identical or mirror image situation. Clearly it is better simply to provide all views so as to avoid this question arising in the first place.

Consistency between and among views. The applicant must ensure that each view is entirely consistent with each of the other views. Saying this in another way, it is absolutely necessary that it be physically possible to construct an actual three-dimensional article which would appear, from each appropriate point of view, exactly like what is shown in the various figures.

Supplemental Content. As was mentioned in the previous article, the USPTO e-filing system often degrades drawings so that what appears in IFW (Image File Wrapper) is of notably poorer quality than the drawings originally filed by the applicant. Fortunately the designers of the e-filing system made a provision for storage and retrieval of the image files that were originally e-filed. Such image files are stored in a system called Supplemental Complex Repository for Examiners (SCORE). Applicants can see the content of SCORE by clicking on the "supplemental content" tab in PAIR. Here is an example from an actual design patent application:

29/228,578	TRANSPARENT PROJECTILE DEFEATING SHIELD								STS.D-001	
Select New Case	Applications by Customer	Application Data	Transaction History	Image File Wrapper	Fees	Published Documents	Address & Attorney/Agent	Supplemental Content	Assignments	D Ref

Available Supplemental Content by File Types

This page gives you information about the number of sequences, metatables and other types of supplemental content items associated with the application you requested. Select a link below to obtain version listings and/or download specific files.

Supplemental Content File Types	Quantity
🛈 Sequences	0
🛈 Megatables	0
🛈 Search Results	0
🛈 Computer Program Listings (CPL)	0
🛈 Other Supplemental Content Items	5

It is important that the US practitioner be aware that SCORE exists and that it can be used to overcome problems.

As one example, an examiner might find fault with a drawing in IFW, opining that the drawing is unclear. Yet if the applicant were to attempt to amend the patent application by means of a newly prepared replacement drawing, the examiner is likely to refuse to enter the amendment on the ground that it supposedly adds "new matter".

When problems like this arise, the practitioner should check SCORE to see whether the originally filed drawings are clear (meaning that the problem with the drawings in IFW is not the applicant's fault but is instead due to degradation in the USPTO e-filing system). The attention of the examiner can then be drawn to the originally filed drawings in SCORE. This may for example overcome the examiner's initial refusal to enter the amendment if (with reference to SCORE) it develops that the amendment is not after all presenting "new matter".

Sending drawings to practitioners outside of the US for purposes of design filings in patent offices outside of the US. When a US design patent application is intended to serve as a priority application (under Article 4 of the Paris Convention) in a patent office outside of the US, one of the necessary steps to be carried out by the US practitioner is to send drawings to a practitioner who will file the application in that office.

The quick and easy way to do this is to log into the PAIR system, to click on the IFW tab, and to download as a PDF file the drawings (and perhaps the entire patent application) as they appear in IFW. The problem with this approach is that the drawings in IFW may have been (and probably have been) degraded in the e-filing system. They may also have been "squeezed" to fit into the IFW system, so that (as mentioned in the previous article) for example a square may become a rectangle and a circle may become an ellipse. Such drawings should not be used for foreign filing.

One way to avoid this problem is to file the PDF files that were originally uploaded to the USPTO e-filing system and to send *those* files (not the files from IFW) to foreign counsel. If, however, those original PDF files cannot be found, then the image files from SCORE are likely to serve the purpose much better than the drawings from IFW.

···

It is hoped that these comments will be helpful to design applicants in the USPTO.

Carl Oppedahl
Oppedahl Patent Law Firm LLC
www.oppedahl.com

UNITED STATES
PATENT AND
TRADEMARK OFFICE

Guide for Preparation of Patent Drawings

June 2002

TABLE OF CONTENTS

This page is intentionally blank.

OVERVIEW

This edition of the *Guide for the Preparation of Patent Drawings* replaces the edition published in October 1993.

Eighteen-month (pre-grant) publication of utility and plant applications has led to major changes in the way utility and plant drawings are processed by the United States Patent and Trademark Office (USPTO). See the section titled PROCESSING OF DRAWINGS, beginning on Page 3.

The section titled SELECTED U.S. RULES OF PRACTICE RELATING TO PATENT DRAWINGS, beginning on Page 7, shows Title 35, United States Code, Section 113 and the drawing rules from Title 37, Code of Federal Regulations. In some instances the rule is followed by additional information under the heading *COMMENTS*.

With respect to the review of drawings in the U.S. national stage of international applications, Appendix 1 shows Manual of Patent Examining Procedure (MPEP) 1893.03(f) (Drawings and PCT Rule 11).

With respect to Patent Cooperation Treaty drawing rules, Appendix 2 shows PCT Article 7 (The Drawings), PCT Rule 7 (The Drawings), and relevant portions of PCT Rule 11 (Physical Requirements of the International Application).

Conventional symbols are discussed and shown in Appendix 3.

Appendix 4 presents examples of drawings, each of which serves to illustrate one or more of the drawing standards set forth in 37 CFR 1.84.

Appendix 5 shows Form PTO-948 (NOTICE OF DRAFTSPERSON'S PATENT DRAWING REVIEW) as revised in April 2002.

This page is intentionally blank.

PROCESSING OF DRAWINGS

- **Review of Drawings by Office of Initial Patent Examination**

Utility drawings and plant drawings should be publication-ready at the time the application is filed.

In utility and plant applications filed on or after November 29, 2000 (other than continued prosecution applications), the Office of Initial Patent Examination (OIPE) will review the drawings at the time of filing to make sure they are of sufficient quality for publication. (Since design applications are not subject to eighteen-month publication, drawings filed in design applications are not reviewed by OIPE.) The procedure for review of drawings in the Office of Initial Patent Examination is described in Section 507 of the Manual of Patent Examining Procedure (MPEP), Eighth Edition (August 2001).

The Office will enter the publication-ready drawings, and any replacement drawings that applicant files pursuant to MPEP 507, into an electronic database. When the time for eighteen-month publication comes, the drawings in their electronic form will be used in the creation of the patent application (pre-grant) publication.

After the application has been allowed, the issue fee has been paid, and any new drawing requirements (including any corrections) have been satisfied, the physical drawing sheets will be captured and used in the creation of the patent (grant) publication.

- **Review by Office Draftsperson**

There is no requirement that drawings be reviewed by an Office draftsperson. Drawings will be reviewed by an Office draftsperson only if the examiner seeks the draftsperson's assistance in identifying errors in the drawings.

If an Office draftsperson reviews the drawings and finds that they are unacceptable, the draftsperson should complete a NOTICE OF DRAFTPERSON'S PATENT DRAWING REVIEW (Form PTO-948) and provide it to the examiner.

- **On Examiner's First (Non-Allowance) Action**

The examiner will make sure the drawings are correctly described in the specification's brief description of the drawings and in the specification's detailed description of the invention. See 37 CFR 1.74 on Page 9 of this drawing guide.

If a NOTICE OF DRAFTPERSON'S PATENT DRAWING REVIEW is present in the patent application's file, the notice should be mailed with the examiner's first written communication to the applicant.

If the examiner sees any additional deficiencies in the drawings, he or she should note those deficiencies in an Office action.

Whether the Office's objections to the drawings are indicated on a NOTICE OF DRAFTSPERSON'S PATENT DRAWING REVIEW or in an Office action, the applicant (a) must supply corrected or replacement drawings or (b) must submit proposed drawing corrections in accordance with 37 CFR 1.121(d). In this drawing guide, see Page 42.

- ## On Examiner's Subsequent Actions

The examiner will check to see if a drawing correction was required by a prior Office action and will check to see if the applicant submitted drawings or otherwise replied to the prior requirement.

If, even though there was no prior requirement for drawing corrections, the applicant voluntarily submits new drawings: The examiner will acknowledge receipt of the new drawings and will state whether they are substantively acceptable. If the new drawings are unacceptable the examiner will explain his/her objections. Such explanation may be made by means of a reference to an attached NOTICE OF DRAFTSPERSON'S PATENT DRAWING REVIEW.

If, in response a prior requirement for drawing corrections, the applicant submits a proposal for drawing corrections: See 37 CFR 1.121(d) on Page 42 of this drawing guide. The examiner will review the proposed corrections and will determine if the red-ink changes to the drawings are acceptable and satisfy any earlier requirements set by the examiner. If the changes are approved by the examiner, the applicant will be notified via an OFFICE ACTION SUMMARY FORM (PTO-326). This form will state that the corrected drawings are required in response to the Office action. If the proposed changes are not approved by the examiner, the applicant will be notified via the next Office action, which will include an explanation of the reasons for the disapproval. The applicant will be required to file corrected drawings in response to the Office action to avoid abandonment of the application.

If, in response to a prior requirement for drawing corrections, the applicant submits corrected drawings that are acceptable to the examiner: The applicant will be so notified via the next Office action.

If, in response to a prior requirement for drawing corrections, the applicant submits corrected drawings that are unacceptable to the examiner: The applicant will be so notified via the next Office action, which will include an explanation of the reasons for the unacceptability. The applicant will be required to file corrected drawings in response to the Office action.

If, in response to a prior requirement for drawing corrections, the applicant submits an argument that the drawing requirement was improper: If the argument is not persuasive, the examiner will reply with an explanation of why the requirement is appropriate. The applicant will be required to file corrected drawings in reply to the Office action. If the argument is persuasive, the examiner will so state in the reply and will vacate the drawing requirement.

If, in response to a prior requirement for drawing corrections, the applicant submits a request that the drawing requirement be held in abeyance with neither drawings nor proposed drawing corrections: The examiner will hold that the request is not responsive to the requirement. See 37 CFR 1.85(a) on Page 38 of this drawing guide.

If, in response to a final Office action, the applicant submits a request for continued examination (RCE), but neither drawing corrections nor an argument that the drawing requirement was improper, and the period for reply to the action has run: The examiner will hold the RCE improper because the reply was not a *bona fide* reply, and hold the application to be abandoned.

- On Allowance

Status of proposed drawing correction or of new drawings: If the examiner has not previously provided such an indication, the examiner will indicate the acceptability or unacceptability of any proposed drawing correction or any new drawings.

Specification's brief description of the drawings: If drawings have been added or amended, the examiner should check the specification's brief description of the drawings to make sure that there is a brief description of each drawing and that each drawing described in the specification has been accepted and included in the file. The specification must be amended if the brief description of the drawings has been omitted or is incorrect. It should be noted that when the drawing sheets show partial views or subdivided views (that is, views that share the same Arabic numeral), it is acceptable for the specification's brief description of the drawings to state the figure number by Arabic numeral only. For example, the drawing sheets may show FIG. 6A and FIG. 6B, but it is acceptable for the brief description to read "FIG. 6 shows … ." However, if the brief description does identify FIG. 6A, then it must also identify FIG. 6B, and must be amended accordingly if it does not do so.

If applicant has indicated that drawings are informal: If the applicant has indicated that the drawings submitted on filing were informal, the examiner will <u>not</u> for that reason alone set a requirement that "formal" drawings be submitted.

If the Notice of Allowability requires the applicant to file corrected or new drawings: The examiner will properly mark the Notice of Allowability when a drawing correction requirement or a new drawing requirement is being set at the time of allowance. The applicant must submit the required drawings within three months of the mail date of the Notice of Allowability, which sets the requirement. This response period cannot be extended. If the required drawings are not timely submitted by the end of the three-month response period, the application will be abandoned. See 37 CFR 1.85(c) on Page 38 of this drawing guide.

- **After Allowance**

The allowed application, including any drawings, will be forwarded to the Office of Patent Publication. Drawings submitted during the post-allowance period will be forwarded to the Office of Patent Publication.

If the Office of Patent Publication receives drawings that cannot be optically scanned or that are otherwise unacceptable for publication: The Office of Patent Publication will inform the applicant by mail that a new requirement for corrected drawings has been set. The applicant must submit the corrected drawings within two months of the mail date of the requirement. This two-month response period cannot be extended.

If an applicant who has already met the drawing requirement chooses to voluntarily submit new drawings after allowance and after payment of the issue fee: The Office of Patent Publication may or may not capture and publish such drawings as part of the patent, depending upon the expediency with which these new drawings can be processed and provided that an amendment to the brief or detailed description of the drawings to correspond to the new figure(s) if required, is also filed.

Fax submission of drawings with faxed payment of the issue fee: The USPTO *sua sponte* waived the prohibition in 37 CFR 1.6(d)(4) against the submission of drawings by facsimile transmission with the issue fee. See the notice entitled *Payment of the Issue Fee and Filing Related Correspondence by Facsimile*, 1254 Off. Gaz. Pat. Office 91 (January 15, 2002). Applicants should still consider the type of drawing in terms of reproducibility by the receiving facsimile machine, recognizing that the quality of the drawings may be affected by the transmission process, before deciding to transmit drawings to the USPTO by facsimile transmission. Should the USPTO receive an unacceptable reproduction, applicants will be so informed and given an opportunity to resubmit acceptable corrected drawings by mail. Fax drawings should be submitted with the payment of the issue fee to (703) 746-4000.

SELECTED U.S. LAWS AND RULES OF PRACTICE
RELATING TO PATENT DRAWINGS

---

from

United States Code Title 35—Patents

PART II—PATENTABILITY OF INVENTIONS AND GRANT OF PATENTS

Chapter 11—APPLICATION FOR PATENT

---

35 U.S.C. 113   Drawings.

The applicant shall furnish a drawing where necessary for the understanding of the subject matter sought to be patented. When the nature of such subject matter admits of illustration by a drawing and the applicant has not furnished such a drawing, the Director may require its submission within a time period of not less than two months from the sending of a notice thereof. Drawings submitted after the filing date of the application may not be used (i) to overcome any insufficiency of the specification due to lack of an enabling disclosure or otherwise inadequate disclosure therein, or (ii) to supplement the original disclosure thereof for the purpose of interpretation of the scope of any claim.

37 CFR 1.58   **Chemical and mathematical formulae and tables.**

(a) The specification, including the claims, may contain chemical and mathematical formulas, but shall not contain drawings or flow diagrams. The description portion of the specification may contain tables; claims may contain tables ...

. . .

COMMENTS

Under 37 CFR 1.58 the specification may <u>not</u> contain drawings, flow charts, graphs, waveforms, etc.

Under 37 CFR 1.58 the specification may contain chemical formulas, mathematical equations, and tables.

Under 37 CFR 1.84(d) chemical formulas, mathematical equations, and tables may be submitted as drawings. See Page 17.

37 CFR 1.74   Reference to drawings.

When there are drawings, there shall be a brief description of the several views of the drawings and the detailed description of the invention shall refer to the different views by specifying the numbers of the figures and to the different parts by use of reference letters or numerals (preferably the latter).

from

Title 37—Code of Federal Regulations
Patents, Trademarks, and Copyrights

CHAPTER I—PATENT AND TRADEMARK OFFICE,
DEPARTMENT OF COMMERICE

PART 1—RULES OF PRACTICE IN PATENT CASES

Subpart B—National Processing Provisions

THE DRAWINGS

37 CFR 1.81   Drawings required in patent application.

(a) The applicant for a patent is required to furnish a drawing of his or her invention where necessary for the understanding of the subject matter sought to be patented; this drawing, or a high quality copy thereof, must be filed with the application. Since corrections are the responsibility of the applicant, the original drawing(s) should be retained by the applicant for any necessary future correction.

(b) Drawings may include illustrations, which facilitate an understanding of the invention (for example, flowsheets in cases of processes, and diagrammatic views).

(c) Whenever the nature of the subject matter sought to be patented admits of illustration by a drawing without its being necessary for the understanding of the subject matter and the applicant has not furnished such a drawing, the examiner will require its submission within a time period of not less than two months from the date of the sending of a notice thereof.

(d) Drawings submitted after the filing date of the application may not be used to overcome any insufficiency of the specification due to lack of an enabling disclosure or otherwise inadequate disclosure therein, or to supplement the original disclosure thereof for the purpose of interpretation of the scope of any claim.

37 CFR 1.83   Content of drawing.

(a) The drawing in a nonprovisional application must show every feature of the invention specified in the claims. However, conventional features disclosed in the description and claims, where their detailed illustration is not essential for a proper understanding of the invention, should be illustrated in the drawing in the form of a graphical drawing symbol or a labeled representation (e.g., a labeled rectangular box).

(b) When the invention consists of an improvement on an old machine the drawing must when possible exhibit, in one or more views, the improved portion itself, disconnected from the old structure, and also in another view, so much only of the old structure as will suffice to show the connection of the invention therewith.

(c) Where the drawings in a nonprovisional application do not comply with the requirements of paragraphs (a) and (b) of this section, the examiner shall require such additional illustration within a time period of not less than two months from the date of the sending of a notice thereof. Such corrections are subject to the requirements of § 1.81(d).

37 CFR 1.84(a)   Standards for drawings

(a)   *Drawings.* There are two acceptable categories for presenting drawings in utility and design patent applications:

(1) **Black ink.** Black and white drawings are normally required. India ink, or its equivalent that secures solid black lines, must be used for drawings; or

(2) **Color.** On rare occasions, color drawings may be necessary as the only practical medium by which to disclose the subject matter sought to be patented in a utility or design patent application or the subject matter of a statutory invention registration. The color drawings must be of sufficient quality such that all details in the drawings are reproducible in black and white in the printed patent. Color drawings are not permitted in international applications (see PCT Rule 11.13), or in an application, or copy thereof, submitted under the Office electronic filing system. The Office will accept color drawings in utility or design patent applications and statutory invention registrations only after granting a petition filed under this paragraph explaining why the color drawings are necessary. Any such petition must include the following:

(i) The fee set forth in § 1.17(h);

(ii) Three (3) sets of color drawings;

(iii) A black and white photocopy that accurately depicts, to the extent possible, the subject matter shown in the color drawing; and

(iv) An amendment to the specification to insert (unless the specification contains or has been previously amended to contain) the following language as the first paragraph of the brief description of the drawings:

> The patent or application file contains at least one drawing executed in color. Copies of this patent or patent application publication with color drawing(s) will be provided by the Office upon request and payment of the necessary fee.

37 CFR 1.84(a) [COMMENTS]

COMMENTS

See the notice titled *Interim Waiver of Parts of 37 CFR 1.84 and 1.165, and Delay in the Enforcement of the Change in 37 CFR 1.84(e) to No Longer Permit Mounting of Photographs*, **as published in the** *Official Gazette* **on May 22, 2001 (1246 OG 106):**

- **WAIVER:** The Office has waived the requirement set forth in 37 CFR 1.84(a)(2)(iii) and 1.165(b) by which the applicant was to file a black and white photocopy of a color drawing or color photograph. The black and white photocopy of the color drawing or color photograph is not required.

In general, "black ink" drawings must be prepared with the aid of drafting instruments.

The Office will also accept computer-generated "black ink" drawings provided that the drawings are substantially equivalent in quality to drawings made with drafting instruments. The jagged and wavy lines characteristic of some computer- generated drawing systems must be kept to an absolute minimum. The artwork in drawings submitted to the Office should be of a professional quality.

The "black ink" drawing may a computer screen image when such an image is necessary for the understanding of the invention.

When color drawings are accepted after the granting of a petition, the three sets are distributed as follows:

- **One set remains in the patent application file wrapper.**

- **One set is included within the official grant of the Letters Patent for routing to the applicant.**

- **One set is maintained in the Office of Public Records, Document Services Division, and is to be used for color-copying purposes when the Office of Public Records sells color copies of the patent for the fee set forth in 37 CFR 1.19(a)(2) or (3).**

In patent application publications, the drawings are published in black and white, even when the applicant has filed color drawings. In utility and design patents and statutory invention registrations, the drawings are published in black and white, even when the applicant has filed color drawings, except (as described above) any color drawings will be included in the official grant of the Letters Patent and in color copies of the patent sold by the Office of Public Records. Only the paper copies of plant patents are published in color.

---

37 CFR 1.84(b)

Photographs.

(1) ***Black and white.*** Photographs, including photocopies of photographs, are not ordinarily permitted in utility and design patent applications. The Office will accept photographs in utility and design patent applications, however, if photographs are the only practicable medium for illustrating the claimed invention. For example, photographs or photomicrographs of: electrophoresis gels, blots (*e.g.*, immunological, western, Southern, and northern), autoradiographs, cell cultures (stained and unstained), histological tissue cross sections (stained and unstained), animals, plants, in vivo imaging, thin layer chromatography plates, crystalline structures, and, in a design patent application, ornamental effects, are acceptable. If the subject matter of the application admits of illustration by a drawing, the examiner may require a drawing in place of the photograph. The photographs must be of sufficient quality so that all details in the photographs are reproducible in the printed patent.

(2) ***Color photographs.*** Color photographs will be accepted in utility and design patent applications if the conditions for accepting color drawings and black and white photographs have been satisfied. See paragraphs (a)(2) and (b)(1) of this section.

COMMENTS

Patent practitioners are cautioned that photographs cannot be removed from applications pending in the Office. Therefore, practitioners should make sure they retain an original set of photographs.

The Office is willing to accept black-and-white photographs or photomicrographs (not photolithographs or other reproductions of photographs made by using screens) developed on photographic paper in lieu of ink drawings to illustrate inventions which are incapable of being accurately or adequately depicted by ink drawings. The photographs or photomicrographs must show the invention more clearly than it can be shown by ink drawings and otherwise comply with the rules concerning such drawings. Examples of acceptable categories of photographs are listed in the rule.

37 CFR 1.84(b)   [continuation of COMMENTS]

There are instances when photographs are produced through use of equipment such as tunneling electron microscopy (TEM). For example, in areas such as solid state electronics, wherein single atoms or single atomic layers can form part of the invention, only TEM or comparable equipment images can resolve single atoms or radicals. In such instances, the Office will not necessarily object to the images for not being completely sharp as long as the content of such TEMs adds to the understanding of the invention and as long as the TEMs can be adequately reproduced in the printed patent.

Photographs taken with such specialized equipment must meet the same standards as photographs which do not require such specialized equipment. Images produced through use of specialized equipment may not always appear with secure black solid lines. However, the drawing review will consider such limitations and accept full tone photographs that meet the specified requirements.

Although photographs are not mentioned in PCT Rule 11, it is possible for black and white photographs to appear as drawings in an international application. In part, MPEP 1825 states the following:

> **The PCT makes no provision for photographs. Nevertheless, they are allowed by the International Bureau where it is impossible to present in a drawing what is to be shown (for instance, crystalline structures). Where, exceptionally, photographs are submitted, they must be on sheets of A4 size, they must be black and white, and they must respect the minimum margins and admit of direct reproduction. Color photographs are not accepted.**

In the U.S. national stage, the Office will accept the photographs that have been approved in the international application. Since MPEP 1893.03(f) prohibits the Office from imposing requirements beyond those in PCT Rule 11, it is not necessary for national stage cases to meet the petition requirement or three-set requirement set forth in 37 CFR 1.84(b). See Appendix 1 and Appendix 2.

The Office will object to mounted photographs. See Page 18.

The Office will not object if photographs are submitted on shiny or glossy paper. See Page 18.

The Office has waived the requirement that the applicant submit a black and white photocopy of a color photograph. See Page 13.

---

37 CFR 1.84(c)

(c) *Identification of drawings.* Identifying indicia, if provided, should include the title of the invention, inventor's name, and application number, or docket number (if any) if an application number has not been assigned to the application. If this information is provided, it must be placed on the front of each sheet and centered within the top margin.

COMMENTS

Although identifying indicia are not required and although the absence of such indicia will not be the basis of an objection, nevertheless the Office does strongly encourage applicants to provide such identifying information so that the Office can match a drawing sheet to the proper application. Indicia, if provided on the front of the drawings must be placed on the front of each sheet and centered within the top margin so that electronic and paper copies of the drawings will include the indicia. If indicia is placed on the back of the drawings, the drawings will not be objected to, but electronic and paper copies of the drawings will not have the benefit of the indicia.

In a drawing that appears in the U.S. national stage of an international application filed under the Patent Cooperation Treaty, the top of the drawing sheet may show the international publication number and publication date. This is not objectionable under 37 CFR 1.84(c).

---

37 CFR 1.84(d)

(d) *Graphic forms in drawings.* Chemical or mathematical formulae, tables, and waveforms may be submitted as drawings and are subject to the same requirements as drawings. Each chemical or mathematical formula must be labeled as a separate figure, using brackets when necessary, to show that information is properly integrated. Each group of waveforms must be presented as a single figure, using a common vertical axis with time extending along the horizontal axis. Each individual waveform discussed in the specification must be identified with a separate letter designation adjacent to the vertical axis.

COMMENTS

See Page 8. Under 37 CFR 1.58 chemical formulas, mathematical equations, and tables may be included in the specification. However, the specification may not contain flow diagrams, waveforms, graphs, etc., which must be submitted as drawings.

If a computer program listing is 300 or fewer lines and each line is 72 or fewer characters, the listing may be submitted as drawings. See 37 CFR 1.96 on Pages 40+41.

Nucleotide and/or amino acid sequence data may be submitted as drawings, but the application is nevertheless subject to the Sequence Listing rules set forth in 37 CFR 1.821 through 1.825,that is, the applicant must submit computer readable form, etc.,if the application (including the drawings) contains "an unbranched sequence of four or more amino acids or an unbranched sequence of ten or more nucleotides."

---

37 CFR 1.84(e)

(e) *Type of paper.* Drawings submitted to the Office must be made on paper which is flexible, strong, white, smooth, non-shiny, and durable. All sheets must be reasonably free from cracks, creases, and folds. Only one side of the sheet may be used for the drawing. Each sheet must be reasonably free from erasures and must be free from alterations, overwritings, and interlineations. Photographs must be developed on paper meeting the sheet-size requirements of paragraph (f) of this section and the margin requirements of paragraph (g) of this section. See paragraph (b) of this section for other requirements for photographs.

COMMENTS

See the notice titled *Interim Waiver of Parts of 37 CFR 1.84 and 1.165, and Delay in the Enforcement of the Change in 37 CFR 1.84(e) to No Longer Permit Mounting of Photographs*, as published in the *Official Gazette* on May 22, 2001 (1246 OG 106).

- **PARTIAL WAIVER:** 37 CFR 1.84(e) requires that drawings be submitted on non-shiny paper. While the Office continues to require that line drawings be submitted on non-shiny paper, the Office will not object if photographs are submitted on shiny or glossy paper. See *COMMENTS* under 37 CFR 1.165(b) on Page 46.

- **ENFORCEMENT DELAYED BUT NOW IN EFFECT:** As of October 1, 2001, the Office will object to mounted photographs. 37 CFR 1.84(e) precludes the mounting of photographs. However, some applicants continued to file mounted photographs after the rule went into effect on November 29, 2000. Instead of requiring "applicants to obtain costly unmounted replacements" and in order "to allow applicants more time to explore alternative options (e.g., use of digital cameras or development options resulting in a digital image)," the Office delayed enforcement of the rule until October 1, 2001.

The requirement that the drawing be "reasonably free" from erasures, alterations, etc., is set forth so that, upon reproduction in the printed patent grant, the drawing will be clear and understandable.

In the interest of protecting the drawings, practitioners are encouraged to transmit drawings by mail so that they are (1) protected by a sheet of heavy binder's board or (2) hand-carried to the Office. Drawings should never be folded. Drawings may be faxed with payment of the issue fee (see Page 6); however, the quality of some drawings may be deteriorated by the faxing process.

---

37 CFR 1.84(f)

(f) *Size of paper.* All drawing sheets in an application must be the same size. One of the shorter sides of the sheet is regarded as its top. The size of the sheets on which drawings are made must be:

(1) 21.0 cm. by 29.7 cm. (DIN size A4), or

(2) 21.6 cm. by 27.9 cm. (8½ by 11 inches).

COMMENTS

PCT Rule 11.5 states that the International Bureau's record copy of an international application must be size A4. Since the International Bureau provides the copies of drawings for the national stage to the designated offices, the drawing sheets in the U.S. national stage of an international application will be size A4. See Appendix 2.

---

37 CFR 1.84(g)

(g) *Margins.* The sheets must not contain frames around the sight (*i.e.*, the usable surface), but should have scan target points (*i.e.*, cross-hairs) printed on two cater-corner margin corners. Each sheet must include a top margin of at least 2.5 cm. (1 inch), a left side margin of at least 2.5 cm. (1 inch), a right side margin of at least 1.5 cm. (5/8 inch), and a bottom margin of at least 1.0 cm. (3/8 inch), thereby leaving a sight no greater than 17.0 cm. by 26.2 cm. on 21.0 cm. by 29.7 cm. (DIN size A4) drawing sheets, and a sight no greater than 17.6 cm. by 24.4 cm. (6 15/16 by 9 5/8 inches) on 21.6 cm. by 27.9 cm. (8½ by 11 inch) drawing sheets.

COMMENTS

Scan target points facilitate the scanning and printing of the patent drawings and are desirable in light of the different sights on the two acceptable sheet sizes. 37 CFR 1.84(g) says that the drawing sheets "should" have these scan target points, which indicates that the Office is stating a preference and will not object to the absence of the scan target points.

See PCT Rule 11.6(e) on Page A-2-4 of Appendix 2. This rule states that "the margins of the international application ... must be completely blank." It has been suggested that scan target points are in conflict with this rule. As indicated above, the applicant may elect not to place scan target points on the drawing sheets. Otherwise, an applicant filing drawings that were previously filed in an international application may add the scan target points only to the copies of the drawing sheets being filed in the Office. Similarly, an applicant filing drawings that will later be filed as part of an international application may place scan target points only on the copies of the drawings being filed in the Office.

---

37 CFR 1.84(h)

(h) *Views.* The drawing must contain as many views as necessary to show the invention. The views may be plan, elevation, section, or perspective views. Detail views of portions of elements, on a larger scale if necessary, may also be used. All views of the drawing must be grouped together and arranged on the sheet(s) without wasting space, preferably in an upright position, clearly separated from one another, and must not be included in the sheets containing the specifications, claims, or abstract. Views must not be connected by projection lines and must not contain center lines. Waveforms of electrical signals may be connected by dashed lines to show the relative timing of the waveforms.

(1) *Exploded views.* Exploded views, with the separated parts embraced by a bracket, to show the relationship or order of assembly of various parts are permissible. When an exploded view is shown in a figure which is on the same sheet as another figure, the exploded view should be placed in brackets.

(2) *Partial views.* When necessary, a view of a large machine or device in its entirety may be broken into partial views on a single sheet, or extended over several sheets if there is no loss in facility of understanding the view. Partial views drawn on separate sheets must always be capable of being linked edge to edge so that no partial view contains parts of another partial view. A smaller scale view should be included showing the whole formed by the partial views and indicating the positions of the parts shown. When a portion of a view is enlarged for magnification purposes, the view and the enlarged view must each be labeled as separate views.

(i) Where views on two or more sheets form, in effect, a single complete view, the views on the several sheets must be so arranged that the complete figure can be assembled without concealing any part of any of the views appearing on the various sheets.

(ii) A very long view may be divided into several parts placed one above the other on a single sheet. However, the relationship between the different parts must be clear and unambiguous.

37 CFR 1.84(h) [continued]

(3) *Sectional views.* The plane upon which a sectional view is taken should be indicated on the view from which the section is cut by a broken line. The ends of the broken line should be designated by Arabic or Roman numerals corresponding to the view number of the sectional view, and should have arrows to indicate the direction of sight. Hatching must be used to indicate section portions of an object, and must be made by regularly spaced oblique parallel lines spaced sufficiently apart to enable the lines to be distinguished without difficulty. Hatching should not impede the clear reading of the reference characters and lead lines. If it is not possible to place reference characters outside the hatched area, the hatching may be broken off wherever reference characters are inserted. Hatching must be at a substantial angle to the surrounding axes or principal lines, preferably 45°. A cross section must be set out and drawn to show all of the materials as they are shown in the view from which the cross section was taken. The parts in cross section must show proper material(s) by hatching with regularly spaced parallel oblique strokes, the space between strokes being chosen on the basis of the total area to be hatched. The various parts of a cross section of the same item should be hatched in the same manner and should accurately and graphically indicate the nature of the material(s) that is illustrated in cross section. The hatching of juxtaposed different elements must be angled in a different way. In the case of large areas, hatching may be confined to an edging drawn around the entire inside of the outline of the area to be hatched.   Different types of hatching should have different conventional meanings as regards the nature of a material seen in cross section.

(4) *Alternate position.* A moved position may be shown by a broken line superimposed upon a suitable view if this can be done without crowding; otherwise, a separate view must be used for this purpose.

(5) *Modified forms.* Modified forms of construction must be shown in separate views.

37 CFR 1.84(h) *[COMMENTS]*

COMMENTS

With respect to 37 CFR 1.84(h)(3), section lines should be designated by numbers corresponding to the view number and not by letters.

Hatching as described in 37 CFR 1.84(h)(3) and shading as described in 37 CFR 1.84(m) are not the same technique:

- Hatching is used in cross-sectional views to show "section portions of an object" and consists of "regularly spaced oblique parallel lines." Sometimes a particular form of hatching (see Appendix 3) denotes the material of which a section portion is made.

- Shading (see Page 28) is used in perspective views to indicate the "surface or shape of spherical, cylindrical, and conical elements of an object," although "Flat parts may also be lightly shaded." Spaced lines are preferred for shading, although stippling and other techniques may be used.

Example 6 in Appendix 4 shows a use of hatching that is an exception to 37 CFR 1.84(h)(3).

---

37 CFR 1.84(i)

(i) *Arrangement of views.* One view must not be placed upon another or within the outline of another. All views on the same sheet should stand in the same direction and, if possible, stand so that they can be read with the sheet held in an upright position. If views wider than the width of the sheet are necessary for the clearest illustration of the invention, the sheet may be turned on its side so that the top of the sheet, with the appropriate top margin to be used as the heading space, is on the right-hand side. Words must appear in a horizontal, left-to-right fashion when the page is either upright or turned so that the top becomes the right side, except for graphs utilizing standard scientific convention to denote the axis of abscissas (of X) and the axis of ordinates (of Y).

COMMENTS

One view is not to be superimposed within the outline of another. The requirement that "Words ... appear in a horizontal, left-to-right fashion when the page is either upright or turned so that the top becomes the right side ..." expands the possibilities for presenting graphs to conform to standard scientific conventions, while using a format compatible with automated patent searching displays, such that drawings can be viewed on a monitor in such a manner that words/numbers appear either in the upright position or rotated 90° to the right.

---

37 CFR 1.84(j)

(j) *Front page view.* The drawing must contain as many views as necessary to show the invention. One of the views should be suitable for inclusion on the front page of the patent application publication and patent as the illustration of the invention. Views must not be connected by projection lines and must not contain center lines. Applicant may suggest a single view (by figure number) for inclusion on the front page of the patent application publication and patent.

COMMENTS

Although the applicant may suggest a "front page" figure, the Office may decide that another figure will better illustrate the invention on the patent application publication's front page or on the patent's front page. As stated in the preamble to the final rulemaking titled *Changes to Implement Eighteen-Month Publication of Patent Applications*, **1239 Off. Gaz. Pat. Office 63+96 (October 10, 2000):**

> **. . . Section 1.84(j) is . . . amended to provide that: (1) One of the views should be suitable for inclusion on the front page of the patent application publication and patent as illustration of the invention; and (2) applicant may suggest a single view (by figure number) for inclusion on the front page of the patent application publication and patent. Applicants should indicate in the application transmittal letter the figure number of the view suggested for inclusion on the front page of the patent application publication and patent. The Office, however, is not bound by the applicant's suggestion. . . .**

The view that is shown on the front page of the patent will also be shown in the *Official Gazette* for patents. (There is no *Official Gazette* for patent application publications.)

The selected view should be at a scale that will clearly illustrate details after being subjected to as much as two-thirds reduction. See 37 CFR 1.84(k).

---

37 CFR 1.84(k)

(k) *Scale.* The scale to which a drawing is made must be large enough to show the mechanism without crowding when the drawing is reduced in size to two-thirds in reproduction. Indications such as "actual size" or "scale ½" on the drawings are not permitted since these lose their meaning with reproduction in a different format.

COMMENTS

Although indications such as "actual size" or "scale ½" are not allowed, measurement indications such as " ←1 inch→ " or " ↙45°↘ " are acceptable.

---

37 CFR 1.84(l)

(l) *Character of lines, numbers, and letters.* All drawings must be made by a process, which will give them satisfactory reproduction characteristics. Every line, number, and letter must be durable, clean, black (except for color drawings), sufficiently dense and dark, and uniformly thick and well-defined. The weight of all lines and letters must be heavy enough to permit adequate reproduction. This requirement applies to all lines however fine, to shading, and to lines representing cut surfaces in sectional views. Lines and strokes of different thicknesses may be used in the same drawing where different thicknesses have a different meaning.

COMMENTS

Use a <u>continuous thick line</u> for edging and outlining views and cross sections.

Use a <u>continuous thin line</u> for leading lines, hatching, outlining parts of adjoining elements, fictitious lines of intersection of surfaces connected by curved or rounded edges.

Use a <u>continuous thin line drawn freehand</u> for delimiting views, part sections, or interrupted views.

Use a <u>thin broken line made up of short dashes</u> for hidden edges and contours.

Use a <u>dot-dash thin line</u> for axes and planes of symmetry, extreme positions of moveable elements, in front of a cross section.

Use a <u>thin line terminating in one heavy line</u> for outlines of cross sections.

---

37 CFR 1.84(m)

(m) *Shading*. The use of shading in views is encouraged if it aids in understanding the invention and if it does not reduce legibility. Shading is used to indicate the surface or shape of spherical, cylindrical, and conical elements of an object. Flat parts may also be lightly shaded. Such shading is preferred in the case of parts shown in perspective, but not for cross sections. See paragraph (h)(3) of this section. Spaced lines for shading are preferred. These lines must be thin, as few in number as practicable, and they must contrast with the rest of the drawings. As a substitute for shading, heavy lines on the shade side of objects can be used except where they superimpose on each other or obscure reference characters. Light should come from the upper left corner at an angle of 45°. Surface delineations should preferably be shown by proper shading. Solid black shading areas are not permitted, except when used to represent bar graphs or color.

COMMENTS

Shading as described in 37 CFR 1.84(m) and hatching as described in 37 CFR 1.84(h)(3) are not the same technique:

- Shading is used in perspective views to indicate the "surface or shape" of an element. Spaced lines (see Example 16 in Appendix 4) are preferred for shading, although stippling (see Example 17 in Appendix 4) and other techniques may be used.

- Hatching (see Pages 22 and 23) is used in cross-sectional views to show "section portions of an object" and consists of "regularly spaced oblique parallel lines." Sometimes a particular form of hatching (see Appendix 3) denotes the material of which a section portion is made.

---

37 CFR 1.84(n)

(n) *Symbols.* Graphical drawing symbols may be used for conventional elements when appropriate. The elements for which such symbols and labeled representations are used must be adequately identified in the specification. Known devices should be illustrated by symbols which have a universally recognized conventional meaning and are generally accepted in the art. Other symbols which are not universally recognized may be used, subject to approval by the Office, if they are not likely to be confused with existing conventional symbols, and if they are readily identifiable.

COMMENTS

See Appendix 3.

---

37 CFR 1.84(o)

(o) *Legends.* Suitable descriptive legends may be used subject to approval by the Office, or may be required by the examiner where necessary for understanding of the drawing. They should contain as few words as possible.

COMMENTS

Words should not be used to describe the figure itself, such as "This is a bar graph."

All text legends must be approved by the Office.

The elements for which such labeled representations are used must be adequately identified in the specification.

Drawings cannot contain the following:

- Expressions or depictions contrary to morality.

- Expressions or depictions contrary to public order.

- Trademarks and service marks unless the applicant is shown to have a proprietary interest in the mark.

- Any statement or other matter obviously irrelevant or unnecessary under the circumstances.

The "as few words as possible" guideline does <u>not</u> apply when the drawing is a computer screen image. See Example 2 in Appendix 4.

---

37 CFR 1.84(p)

(p) *Numbers, letters, and reference characters.*

(1) Reference characters (numerals are preferred), sheet numbers, and view numbers must be plain and legible, and must not be used in association with brackets or inverted commas, or enclosed within outlines, *e.g.*, encircled. They must be oriented in the same direction as the view so as to avoid having to rotate the sheet. Reference characters should be arranged to follow the profile of the object depicted.

(2) The English alphabet must be used for letters, except where another alphabet is customarily used, such as the Greek alphabet to indicate angles, wavelengths, and mathematical formulas.

(3) Numbers, letters, and reference characters must measure at least .32 cm. (1/8 inch) in height. They should not be placed in the drawing so as to interfere with its comprehension. Therefore, they should not cross or mingle with the lines. They should not be placed upon hatched or shaded surfaces. When necessary, such as indicating a surface or cross section, a reference character may be underlined and a blank space may be left in the hatching or shading where the character occurs so that it appears distinct.

(4) The same part of an invention appearing in more than one view of the drawing must always be designated by the same reference character, and the same reference character must never be used to designate different parts.

(5) Reference characters not mentioned in the description shall not appear in the drawings. Reference characters mentioned in the description must appear in the drawings.

37 CFR 1.84(p) [*COMMENTS*]

COMMENTS

Each element on a view must be identified by a reference number, except on design drawings.

While the rules do not specifically prohibit such practices, the use of primed reference characters should be kept to a minimum. Single primed characters for designating the same element in different embodiments, if used sparingly, can aid in easily understanding the invention and its different embodiments, but the overuse of primed numbers tends to obfuscate the drawings and should be avoided. The same holds for subscript and superscript numbers. Although the rules do not specifically prohibit the use of subscripts and superscripts, such use tends to obfuscate the drawing and should be avoided.

---

37 CFR 1.84(q)

(q) *Lead lines.* Lead lines are those lines between the reference characters and the details referred to. Such lines may be straight or curved and should be as short as possible. They must originate in the immediate proximity of the reference character and extend to the feature indicated. Lead lines must not cross each other. Lead lines are required for each reference character except for those, which indicate the surface or cross section on which they are placed. Such a reference character must be underlined to make it clear that a lead line has not been left out by mistake. Lead lines must be executed in the same way as lines in the drawing. See paragraph (l) of this section.

37 CFR 1.84(r)

(r) *Arrows.* Arrows may be used at the ends of lines, provided that their meaning is clear, as follows:

(1) On a lead line, a freestanding arrow to indicate the entire section towards which it points;

(2) On a lead line, an arrow touching a line to indicate the surface shown by the line looking along the direction of the arrow; or

(3) To show the direction of movement.

37 CFR 1.84(s)

(s) *Copyright or Mask Work Notice.* A copyright or mask work notice may appear in the drawing, but must be placed within the sight of the drawing immediately below the figure representing the copyright or mask work material and be limited to letters having a print size of .32 cm. to .64 cm. (Λ to ¼ inches) high. The content of the notice must be limited to only those elements provided for by law. For example, "©1983 John Doe" (17 U.S.C. 401) and "*M* John Doe" (17 U.S.C. 909) would be properly limited and, under current statutes, legally sufficient notices of copyright and mask work, respectively. Inclusion of a copyright or mask work notice will be permitted only if the authorization language set forth in § 1.71(e) is included at the beginning (preferably as the first paragraph) of the specification.

COMMENTS

§ 1.71(d) and § 1.71(e) are reproduced below:

37 CFR 1.71 Detailed description and specification of the invention.

. . .

(d) A copyright or mask work notice may be placed in a design or utility patent application adjacent to copyright and mask work material contained therein. The notice may appear at any appropriate portion of the patent application disclosure. For notices in drawings, see § 1.84(s). The content of the notice must be limited to only those elements provided for by law. For example, "©1983 John Doe (17 U.S.C. 401) and "*M* John Doe" (17 U.S.C. 909) would be properly limited and, under current statutes, legally sufficient notices of copyright and mask work, respectively. Inclusion of a copyright or mask work notice will be permitted only if the authorization language set forth in paragraph (e) of this section is included at the beginning (preferably as the first paragraph) of the specification.

(e) The authorization shall read as follows:

A portion of the disclosure of this patent document contains material, which is subject to (copyright or mask work) protection. The (copyright or mask work) owner has no objection to the facsimile reproduction by anyone of the patent document or the patent disclosure, as it appears in the Patent and Trademark Office patent file or records, but otherwise reserves all (copyright or mask work) rights whatsoever.

---

37 CFR 1.84(t)

(t) *Numbering of sheets of drawings.* The sheets of drawings should be numbered in consecutive Arabic numerals, starting with 1, within the sight as defined in paragraph (g) of this section. These numbers, if present, must be placed in the middle of the top of the sheet, but not in the margin. The numbers can be placed on the right-hand side if the drawing extends too close to the middle of the top edge of the usable surface. The drawing sheet numbering must be clear and larger than the numbers used as reference characters to avoid confusion. The number of each sheet should be shown by two Arabic numerals placed on either side of an oblique line, with the first being the sheet number and the second being the total number of sheets of drawings, with no other marking.

COMMENTS

For example, 2/6 at the top of the sheet would indicate that the sheet is the second sheet of a total of six sheets. If the arrangement of the view is rotated as set forth in 37 CFR 1.84(i), the sheet number must remain as set forth in 37 CFR 1.84(t).

According to PCT Rule 11.7 (see Page A-2-5 of Appendix 2), "All the sheets contained in the international application shall be numbered in consecutive Arabic numerals." That is, the sheets of the request, description, claims, drawings, and abstract will be so numbered. PCT Rule 11.7 further says the sheet numbers can be at either the top or the bottom of the sheet. PCT Rule 11.7 conflicts with 37 CFR 1.84(t)'s separate numbering system for drawing sheets and with 37 CFR 1.84(t)'s "middle of the top" location for sheet numbers. However, under MPEP 1893.03(f) (see Page A-1-1 of Appendix 1), drawings in a national stage case will be accepted by the Office even if the U.S.-style "1/3, 2/3, 3/3" numbering system for drawing sheets is not used and even if the drawing-sheet numbers appear at the bottoms of the sheets.

---

37 CFR 1.84(u)

(u) *Numbering of views.*

(1) The different views must be numbered in consecutive Arabic numerals, starting with 1, independent of the numbering of the sheets and, if possible, in the order in which they appear on the drawing sheet(s). Partial views intended to form one complete view, on one or several sheets, must be identified by the same number followed by a capital letter. View numbers must be preceded by the abbreviation "FIG." Where only a single view is used in an application to illustrate the claimed invention, it must not be numbered and the abbreviation "FIG." must not appear.

(2) Figure numbers and letters identifying the views must be simple and clear and must not be used in association with brackets, circles, or inverted commas. The view numbers must be larger than the numbers used for reference characters.

37 CFR 1.84(v)

(v) *Security markings.* Authorized security markings may be placed on the drawings provided they are outside the sight, preferably centered in the top margin.

COMMENTS

Security markings are primarily the responsibility of the Office; however, the applicant might identify the drawings with the security designations such as NATO, TS, S, or C.

---

37 CFR 1.84(w)

(w) *Corrections.* Any corrections on drawings submitted to the Office must be durable and permanent.

COMMENTS

Special products for corrections, such as white masking fluid, may be used provided they are indelible and comply with all other requirements.

---

37 CFR 1.84(x)

(x) *Holes.* No holes should be made by applicant in the drawing sheets.

37 CFR 1.84(y)

(y) *Types of drawings.* See § 1.152 for design drawings, § 1.165 for plant drawings, and § 1.174 for reissue drawings.

37 CFR 1.85   Corrections to drawings.

(a) A utility or plant application will not be placed on the files for examination until objections to the drawings have been corrected. Except as provided in § 1.215(c), any patent application publication will not include drawings filed after the application has been placed on the files for examination. Unless applicant is otherwise notified in an Office action, objections to the drawings in a utility or plant application will not be held in abeyance, and a request to hold objections to the drawings in abeyance will not be considered a *bona fide* attempt to advance the application to final action (§ 1.135(c)).   If a drawing in a design application meets the requirements of § 1.84(e), (f), and (g) and is suitable for reproduction, but is not otherwise in compliance with § 1.84, the drawing may be admitted for examination.

(b) The Office will not release drawings for purposes of correction. If corrections are necessary, new corrected drawings must be submitted within the time set by the Office.

(c) If a corrected drawing is required or if a drawing does not comply with § 1.84 at the time an application is allowed, the Office may notify the applicant and set a three month period of time from the mail date of the notice of allowability within which the applicant must file a corrected or formal drawing in compliance with § 1.84 to avoid abandonment. This time period is not extendable under § 1.136(a) or § 1.136(b).

37 CFR 1.85 [*COMMENTS*]

COMMENTS

1.85(a) , A utility application or a plant application will not be examined until its drawings are "publication ready" with respect to eighteen-month (pre-grant) publication. See MPEP 507. Objections to drawings will not be held in abeyance. Applicants must submit drawing corrections in reply to an Office drawing requirement to avoid abandonment of the application.

1.85(c) , When the Notice of Allowability sets a requirement for formal or corrected drawings, the applicant must submit the drawings within three months of the mail date of the Notice of Allowability. The applicant cannot extend this reply period. If the drawings are not received within the reply period, the application will be regarded as abandoned. Drawings that are voluntarily submitted by the applicant after allowance and payment of the issue fee may or may not be printed, dependent on the expediency with which these drawings can be processed, provided an amendment to the brief or detailed description of the drawings to correspond to the new figure(s), if required, is also filed. See Pages 5 and 6.

---

from 37 CFR 1.96 Submission of computer program listings.

(a) *General.* Descriptions of the operation and general content of computer program listings should appear in the description portion of the specification. A computer program listing for the purpose of this section is defined as a printout that lists in appropriate sequence the instructions, routines, and other contents of a program for a computer. The program listing may be either in machine or machine-independent (object or source) language which will cause a computer to perform a desired procedure or task such as solve a problem, regulate the flow of work in a computer, or control or monitor events. Computer program listings may be submitted in patent applications as set forth in paragraphs (b) and (c) of this section.

(b) *Material, which will be printed in the patent.* If the computer program listing is contained in 300 lines or fewer, with each line of 72 characters or fewer, it may be submitted either as drawings or as part of the specification.

(1) *Drawings.* If the listing is submitted as drawings, it must be submitted in the manner and complying with the requirements for drawings as provided in § 1.84. At least one figure numeral is required on each sheet of drawing.

from **37 CFR 1.96 [continued]**

    (2) *Specification.*

    (i) . . .

    (ii) Any listing having more than 60 lines of code that is submitted as part of the specification must be positioned at the end of the description but before the claims. Any amendment must be made by way of submission of a substitute sheet.

    (c) *As an appendix which will not be printed*: Any computer program listing may, and any computer program listing having over 300 lines (up to 72 characters per line) must, be submitted on a compact disc in compliance with § 1.52(e) . . .

from **37 CFR 1.121**   **Manner of making amendments in application.**

(a) *Amendments in applications, other than reissue applications.*

. . .

(d) *Drawings.* Application drawings are amended in the following manner: Any change to the application drawings must be submitted on a separate paper showing the proposed changes in red for approval by the examiner. Upon approval by the examiner, new drawings in compliance with § 1.84 including the changes must be filed.

(e) *Disclosure consistency.* The disclosure must be amended, when required by the Office, to correct inaccuracies of description and definition, and to secure substantial correspondence between the claims, the remainder of the specification, and the drawings.

. . .

37 CFR 1.151   Rules applicable.

The rules relating to applications for patents for other inventions or discoveries are also applicable to applications for patents for designs except as otherwise provided.

COMMENTS

This rule is included here to show that unless a design drawing requirement is specifically mentioned in 37 CFR 1.152, the provisions of 37 CFR 1.84 are controlling for the content and quality of drawings for design patent applications.

---

37 CFR 1.152   Design drawings.

The design must be represented by a drawing that complies with the requirements of § 1.84 and must contain a sufficient number of views to constitute a complete disclosure of the appearance of the design. Appropriate and adequate surface shading should be used to show the character or contour of the surfaces represented. Solid black surface shading is not permitted except when used to represent the color black as well as color contrast. Broken lines may be used to show visible environmental structure, but may not be used to show hidden planes and surfaces that cannot be seen through opaque materials. Alternate positions of a design component, illustrated by full and broken lines in the same view are not permitted in a design drawing. Photographs and ink drawings are not permitted to be combined as formal drawings in one application. Photographs submitted in lieu of ink drawings in design patent applications must not disclose environmental structures but must be limited to the design claimed for the article.

37 CFR 1.161   **Rules applicable.**

The rules relating to applications for patent for other inventions or discoveries are also applicable to applications for patents for plants except as otherwise provided.

COMMENTS

This rule is included here to show that unless a plant drawing requirement is specifically mentioned in 37 CFR 1.165, the provisions of 37 CFR 1.84 are controlling for the content and quality of drawings for plant patent applications.

---

37 CFR 1.165   Plant drawings.

(a) Plant patent drawings should be artistically and competently executed and must comply with the requirements of § 1.84. View numbers and reference characters need not be employed unless required by the examiner. The drawing must disclose all the distinctive characteristics of the plant capable of visual representation.

(b) The drawings may be in color. The drawing must be in color if color is a distinguishing characteristic of the new variety. Two copies of color drawings or photographs and a black and white photocopy that accurately depicts, to the extent possible, the subject matter shown in the color drawing or photograph must be submitted.

COMMENTS

See the notice titled *Interim Waiver of Parts of 37 CFR 1.84 and 1.165, and Delay in the Enforcement of the Change in 37 CFR 1.84(e) to No Longer Permit Mounting of Photographs*, as published in the *Official Gazette* on May 22, 2001 (1246 OG 106).

- **WAIVER:** The Office has waived the requirement set forth in 37 CFR 1.84(a)(2)(iii) and 1.165(b) for a black and white photocopy of a color drawing or color photograph. The black and white photocopy of the color drawing or color photograph is <u>not</u> required. See *COMMENTS* under 37 CFR 1.84(a)(2)(iii) on Page 13.

- **PARTIAL WAIVER:** While the Office continues to require that line drawings be submitted on non-shiny paper per 37 CFR 1.84(e), the Office will <u>not</u> object if photographs are submitted on shiny or glossy paper. To quote the above-identified notice: "By requiring drawings (including photographs) for plant patent applications to comply with 37 CFR 1.84, 37 CFR 1.165 suggests that plant patent photographs must not be shiny. Color photographs, however, generally have better color quality when produced with a shiny or gloss finish rather than a matte finish. As a result, the Office will not object to a standard photographic appearance, including a glossy or shiny finish." See *COMMENTS* under 37 CFR 1.84(e) on Page 18.

- **ENFORCEMENT DELAYED BUT NOW IN EFFECT:** As of October 1, 2001, the Office <u>will</u> object to mounted photographs. 37 CFR 1.84(e), effective November 29, 2000, precludes the mounting of photographs. However, some applicants continued to file mounted photographs after November 29, 2000. Because the Office did not want to require "applicants to obtain costly unmounted replacements" and because the Office wanted "to allow applicants more time to explore alternative options (e.g., use of digital cameras or development options resulting in a digital image)," the Office delayed enforcement of the rule until October 1, 2001.

37 CFR 1.165   [continuation of *COMMENTS*]

The terms "drawing" and "photograph" are used interchangeably herein as they are both acceptable means of illustration under 37 CFR 1.165 for plant patent applications filed under 35 U.S.C. 161.

Color drawings may be made either in permanent water color or oil, or in lieu thereof may be photographs made by color photography or properly colored on sensitized paper.

Plant patent drawings must show the most distinguishing characteristics of the plant. Color drawings must reasonably closely correspond to the color values set forth in the specification and must accurately depict the true coloration of the plant parts so illustrated.

Care should be taken to assure that the subject is well centered and clearly in focus. Leaves, stems, flowers, whole and cut fruit (or nuts) may appropriately be shown in various combinations in a single drawing. Distinguishing characteristics occurring at different seasons should be illustrated, and may be depicted in different sheets or figures. Flower and seed parts not particularly distinguishing may still be included (if convenient) for the sake of completeness. Photographic drawings should not be retouched or amended/altered by the addition of color, as such drawings cannot be faithfully reproduced by the printer.

Drawings should avoid the inclusion of superfluous information or material(s) such as tags or stickers (unwarranted and improper advertising) which add little if anything in the way of further definition to the plant. However, scale definition means such as rulers, etc., in intimate proximity to the plant are acceptable. Drawings should be of such scale and clarity that necessary detail can still be discerned even with a fifty percent reduction in scale as may happen upon printing of same should the application mature into a plant patent.

Drawings should not be limited to a single plant part—i.e., the fruit, nut, flower, or leaf as applicable, but should also depict the entire plant, even if the single plant part may be the entirety of what is viewed by applicant as being novel. Where flowers, foliage, fruit, etc. of the claimed plant are not depicted in sufficient scale in a whole plant drawing or view, this view should be supplemented with a close-up view of specific parts. Typical of what is sought and may be necessary on a case-by-case basis in this supplemental view would be:

- **Ornamental flowering plant,Views at bud, early bloom, and late bloom stage showing bloom shapes and character. Flower parts may be shown separated from whole flowers—i.e., to depict color differences between top and bottom surfaces of petals or leaves, differences in coloration of petals from basal to terminal portions, and color and shape differences between petals from**

37 CFR 1.165   [continuation of *COMMENTS*]

different locations of the flower and different ages. Foliage and stems (bark) may also be so depicted. Where there is characteristic variation in leaf shape, each characteristic shape should be depicted. For perennial deciduous plants, the drawing should include a showing of the plant in a dormant state to illustrate details of bark and branching.

- Fruit or nut bearing plant,Views depicted at different attitudes, with fruit (or nut) split in different directions to show details and coloration of seeds, stone, stone well, core, flesh coloration, skin ground coloration, blush and pubescence (as applicable). Bloom may also be shown along with foliage.

Fingerprint information may also be presented as a figure of the drawing and should include identifying information. Such drawings should be given view numbers, as appropriate. These illustrations may be mechanical in nature, or in the case of isozyme banding, be presented as a black-and-white photograph, even if other drawing figures are in color.

Where the pedigree of the plant is disclosed in the form of a detailed flow chart, this must be made a drawing view and not appear in the specification, as per 37 CFR 1.58(a). The printer will not print same in the body of the specification proper.

Where a claimed plant is a sport of a known variety, every effort should be made to photograph the sported plant in a side-by-side relationship with the parental variety and such parental variety should clearly be identified as "Prior Art." This applies to plant parts, such as color sports of flowering plants (e.g., roses or chrysanthemums) or fruit (e.g., apples or nectarines).

Duplicate formal drawings should be filed concurrently with the application papers. Examination of drawings for content, detail, scale, and color fidelity is critical to the effective examination of a 35 U.S.C. 161 plant patent application. Filing of informal or single copies of said drawings will result in delay of prosecution of the application—for example, applications otherwise in condition for allowance will not normally be forwarded to the Publishing Division, Office of Patent Publication, prior to receipt and evaluation of formal drawings. The drawing(s) may be in color and when color is a distinguishing characteristic of the new variety, the drawings must be in color (37 CFR 1.165(b)).

The number of drawing views (and sheets) in plant patent applications should be limited to the minimum number necessary to adequately depict the distinctive botanical characteristics of the claimed patent which are capable of being visually represented (37 CFR 1.165(a)). The views may be given view numbers as appropriate, so long as any view numbers set forth in the drawings find corresponding reference in the written specification.

---

37 CFR 1.171   Application for reissue.

An application for reissue must contain the same parts required for an application for an original patent, complying with all the rules relating thereto except as otherwise provided, and in addition, must comply with the requirements of the rules relating to reissue applications.

from **37 CFR 1.173   Reissue specification, drawings, and amendments.**

(a) *Contents of a reissue application.* An application for reissue must contain the entire specification, including the claims, and the drawings of the patent. No new matter shall be introduced into the application.

. . .

(2) *Drawings.* Applicant must submit a clean copy of each drawing sheet of the printed patent at the time the reissue application is filed. If such copy complies with § 1.84, no further drawings will be required. Where a drawing of the reissue application is to include any changes relative to the patent being reissued, the changes to the drawing must be made in accordance with paragraph (b)(3) of this section. The Office will not transfer the drawings from the patent file to the reissue application.

(b) *Making amendments in a reissue application.* . . .

(3) *Drawings.* Any change to the patent drawings must be submitted as a sketch on a separate paper showing the proposed changes in red for approval by the examiner. Upon approval by the examiner, new drawings in compliance with § 1.84 including the approved changes must be filed. Amended figures must be identified as "Amended," and any added figure must be identified as "New." In the event that a figure is canceled, the figure must be surrounded by brackets and identified as "Canceled."

. . .

(f) *Amendment of disclosure may be required.* The disclosure must be amended, when required by the Office, to correct inaccuracies of description and definition, and to secure substantial correspondence between the claims, the remainder of the specification, and the drawings.

(g) *Amendments made relative to the patent.* All amendments must be made relative to the patent specification, including the claims, and drawings, which are in effect as of the date of filing of the reissue application.

from

Title 37—Code of Federal Regulations
Patents, Trademarks, and Copyrights

CHAPTER I—PATENT AND TRADEMARK OFFICE,
DEPARTMENT OF COMMERICE

PART 1—RULES OF PRACTICE IN PATENT CASES

Subpart B—National Processing Provisions

PUBLICATION OF APPLICATIONS

37 CFR 1.211   Publication of applications.

. . .

(c) . . . The Office may delay publishing any application until it includes a specification having papers in compliance with § 1.52 and an abstract (§ 1.72(b)), drawings in compliance with § 1.84, and a sequence listing in compliance with §§ 1.821 through 1.825 (if applicable), and until any petition under § 1.47 is granted.

37 CFR 1.215   Patent application publication.

(a) . . . The patent application publication will be based upon the application papers deposited on the filing date of the application, as well as the executed oath or declaration submitted to complete the application, or any application papers or drawings submitted in reply to a preexamination notice requiring a title and abstract in compliance with § 1.72, application papers in compliance with § 1.52, drawings in compliance with § 1.84, or a sequence listing in compliance with §§ 1.821 through 1.825, except as otherwise provided in this section. The patent application publication will not include any amendments, including preliminary amendments, unless applicant supplies a copy of the application containing the amendment pursuant to paragraph (c) of this section.

. . .

(c) At applicant's option, the patent application publication will be based upon the copy of the application (specification, drawings, and oath or declaration) as amended during examination, provided that the applicant supplies such a copy in compliance with the Office electronic filing system requirements within one month of the actual filing date of the application or fourteen months of the earliest filing date for which a benefit is sought under title 35, United States Code, whichever is later.

(d) If the copy of the application submitted pursuant to paragraph (c) of this section does not comply with the Office electronic filing system requirements, the Office will publish the application as provided in paragraph (a) of this section. If, however, the Office has not started the publication process, the Office may use an untimely filed copy of the application supplied by the applicant under paragraph (c) of this section in creating the patent application publication.

COMMENTS

See Page 3.

---

37 CFR 1.437   The drawings.

(a) Subject to paragraph (b) of this section, when drawings are necessary for the understanding of the invention, or are mentioned in the description, they must be part of an international application as originally filed in the United States Receiving Office in order to maintain the international filing date during the national stage (PCT Art. 7).

(b) Drawings missing from the application upon filing will be accepted if such drawings are received within 30 days of the date of first receipt of the incomplete papers. If the missing drawings are received within the 30-day period, the international filing date shall be the date on which such drawings are received. If such drawings are not timely received, all references to drawings in the international application shall be considered non-existent (PCT Art. 14(2), Administrative Instruction 310).

(c) The physical requirements for drawings are set forth in PCT Rule 11 and shall be adhered to.

COMMENTS

See Appendix 2.

---

from **37 CFR 1.530**   **Statement by patent owner in *ex parte* reexamination; amendment by patent owner in *ex parte* or *inter partes* reexamination; inventorship change in *ex parte* or *inter partes* reexamination.**

. . .

(d) *Making amendments in a reexamination proceeding.* A proposed amendment in an *ex parte* or an *inter partes* reexamination proceeding is made by filing a paper directing that proposed specified changes be made to the patent specification, including the claims, or to the drawings. . . .

. . .

(3) *Drawings.* Any change to the patent drawings must be submitted as a sketch on a separate paper showing the proposed changes in red for approval by the examiner. Upon approval of the changes by the examiner, only new sheets of drawings including the changes and in compliance with § 1.84 must be filed. Amended figures must be identified as "Amended," and any added figure must be identified as "New." In the event a figure is canceled, the figure must be surrounded by brackets and identified as "Canceled."

from **37 CFR 1.530**   **[continued]**

. . .

(h) *Amendment of disclosure may be required.*   The disclosure must be amended, when required by the Office, to correct inaccuracies of description and definition, and to secure substantial correspondence between the claims, the remainder of the specification, and the drawings.

(i) *Amendments made relative to patent.*   All amendments must be made relative to the patent specification, including the claims, and drawings, which are in effect as of the date of filing the request for reexamination.

. . .

This page is intentionally blank.

Appendix 1

§ 1893.03(f) of Manual of
Patent Examining Procedure

1893.03(f)   **Drawings and PCT Rule 11**

The drawings for the national stage application must comply with PCT Rule 11. The copy of the drawings provided by the International Bureau has already been checked and should be in compliance with PCT Rule 11. Accordingly, the drawing provided by the International Bureau should be acceptable. Sometimes, applicant submits a drawing for use in the national stage application and a check will be made by the Official Draftsman. The Official Draftsman may not impose requirements beyond those imposed by the Patent Cooperation Treaty (e.g., PCT Rule 11). The examiner does indeed have the authority to require new or more acceptable drawings if the drawings were published without meeting all requirements under the PCT for drawings. Unless the applicant requests the use of drawings which he or she has submitted, the drawings to be employed in the national stage are those which are a part of the Article 20 communication.

This page is intentionally blank.

Appendix 2

Article 7 of Patent Cooperation Treaty and Selected PCT Rules Pertaining to Drawings

---

Article 7

The Drawings

(1) Subject to the provisions of paragraph (2)(ii), drawings shall be required when they are necessary for the understanding of the invention.

(2) Where, without being necessary for the understanding of the invention, the nature of the invention admits of illustration by drawings:

(i) the applicant may include such drawings in the international application when filed.

(ii) any designated Office may require that the applicant file such drawings with it within the prescribed time limit.

from Rule 3

The Request (Form)

3.3 *Check List*

(a) The request shall contain a list indicating:

. . .

(iii) the number of that figure of the drawings which the applicant suggests should accompany the abstract when the abstract is published; in exceptional cases, the applicant may suggest more than one figure.

. . .

Rule 7

The Drawings

7.1 *Flow Sheets and Diagrams*

Flowsheets and diagrams are considered drawings.

7.2 *Time Limit*

The time limit referred to in Article 7(2)(ii) shall be reasonable under the circumstances of the case and shall, in no case, be shorter than two months from the date of the written invitation requiring the filing of drawings or additional drawings under the said provision.

from **Rule 8**

The Abstract

8.2 *Figure*

(a) If the applicant fails to make the indication referred to in Rule 3.3(a)(iii), or if the International Searching Authority finds that a figure or figures other than that figure or those figures suggested by the applicant would, among all the figures of all the drawings, better characterize the invention, it shall, subject to paragraph (b), indicate the figure or figures which should accompany the abstract when the latter is published by the International Bureau. In such case, the abstract shall be accompanied by the figure or figures so indicated by the International Searching Authority. Otherwise, the abstract shall, subject to paragraph (b), be accompanied by the figure or figures suggested by the applicant.

(b) If the International Searching Authority finds that none of the figures of the drawings is useful for the understanding of the abstract, it shall notify the International Bureau accordingly. In such case, the abstract, when published by the International Bureau, shall not be accompanied by any figure of the drawings even where the applicant has made a suggestion under Rule 3.3(a)(iii).

from **Rule 9**

Expressions, Etc., Not To Be Used

9.1   *Definition*

The international application shall not contain:

(i) expressions or drawings contrary to morality;

(ii) expressions or drawings contrary to public order;

. . .

from **Rule 11**

**Physical Requirements of the International
Application**

11.2   *Fitness for Reproduction*

(a)   All elements of the international application (i.e., the request, the description, the claims, the drawings, and the abstract) shall be so presented as to admit of direct reproduction by photography, electrostatic processes, photo offset, and microfilming, in any number of copies.

(b)   All sheets shall be free from creases and cracks; they shall not be folded.

(c)   Only one side of each sheet shall be used.

(d)   Subject to . . . Rule 11.13(j), each sheet shall be used in an upright position (i.e., the short sides at the top and bottom).

11.3   *Material to Be Used*

All elements of the international application shall be on paper, which shall be flexible, strong, white, smooth, non-shiny and durable.

from **PCT Rule 11** [continued]

11.4 *Separate Sheets, Etc.*

(a) Each element (request, description, claims, drawings, abstract) of the international application shall commence on a new sheet.

(b) All sheets of the international application shall be so connected that they can be easily turned when consulted, and easily separated and joined again if they have been separated for reproduction purposes.

11.5 *Size of Sheets*

The size of the sheets shall be A4 (29.7 cm × 21 cm). However, any receiving Office may accept international applications on sheets of other sizes provided that the record copy, as transmitted to the International Bureau, and, if the competent International Searching Authority so desires, the search copy, shall be of A4 size.

11.6 *Margins*
   . . .

(c) On sheets containing drawings, the surface usable shall not exceed 26.2 cm × 17.0 cm. The sheets shall not contain frames around the usable or used surface. The minimum margins shall be as follows:
   – top: 2.5 cm
   – left side: 2.5 cm
   – right side: 1.5 cm
   – bottom: 1.0 cm

(d) The margins referred to in paragraphs (a) to (c) apply to A4-size sheets, so that, even if the receiving Office accepts other sizes, the A4-size record copy and, when so required, the A4-size search copy shall leave the aforesaid margins.

(e) Subject to paragraph (f) . . . , the margins of the international application, when submitted, must be completely blank.

from **PCT Rule 11** [continued]

(f)   The top margin may contain in the left-hand corner an indication of the applicant's file reference, provided that the reference appears within 1.5 cm from the top of the sheet. The number of characters in the applicant's file reference shall not exceed the maximum fixed by the Administrative Instructions.

11.7   *Numbering of Sheets*

(a)   All the sheets contained in the international application shall be numbered in consecutive Arabic numerals.

(b)   The numbers shall be centered at the top or bottom of the sheet, but shall not be placed in the margin.

. . .

11.10 *Drawings, Formulae, and Tables, in Text Matter*

(a)   The request, the description, the claims and the abstract shall not contain drawings.

. . .

11.11 *Words in Drawings*

(a)   The drawings shall not contain text matter, except a single word or words, when absolutely indispensable, such as "water," "steam," "open," "closed," "section on AB," and, in the case of electric circuits and block schematic or flow sheet diagrams, a few short catchwords indispensable for understanding.

(b)   Any words used shall be so placed that, if translated, they may be pasted over without interfering with any lines of the drawings.

11.12 *Alterations, Etc.*

Each sheet shall be reasonably free from erasures and shall be free from alterations, overwritings, and interlineations. Non-compliance with this Rule may be authorized if the authenticity of the content is not in question and the requirements for good reproduction are not in jeopardy.

11.13 *Special Requirements for Drawings*

(a) Drawings shall be executed in durable, black, sufficiently dense and dark, uniformly thick and well-defined, lines and strokes without colorings.

(b) Cross-sections shall be indicated by oblique hatching which should not impede the clear reading of the reference signs and leading lines.

(c) The scale of the drawings and the distinctness of their graphical execution shall be such that a photographic reproduction with a linear reduction in size to two-thirds would enable all details to be distinguished without difficulty.

(d) When, in exceptional cases, the scale is given on a drawing, it shall be represented graphically.

(e) All numbers, letters and reference lines, appearing on the drawings, shall be simple and clear. Brackets, circles or inverted commas shall not be used in association with numbers and letters.

(f) All lines in the drawings shall, ordinarily, be drawn with the aid of drafting instruments.

(g) Each element of each figure shall be in proper proportion to each of the other elements in the figure, except where the use of a different proportion is indispensable for the clarity of the figure.

(h) The height of the numbers and letters shall not be less than 0.32 cm. For the lettering of drawings, the Latin and, where customary, the Greek alphabets shall be used.

(i) The same sheet of drawings may contain several figures. Where figures on two or more sheets form in effect a single complete figure, the figures on the several sheets shall be so arranged that the complete figure can be assembled without concealing any part of any of the figures appearing on the various sheets.

(j) The different figures shall be arranged on a sheet or sheets without wasting space, preferably in an upright position, clearly separated from one another. Where the figures are not arranged in an upright position, they shall be presented sideways with the top of the figures at the left side of the sheet.

(k) The different figures shall be numbered in Arabic numerals consecutively and independently of the numbering of the sheets.

(l) Reference signs not mentioned in the description shall not appear in the drawings, and vice versa.

(m) The same features, when denoted by reference signs, shall, throughout the international application, be denoted by the same signs.

(n) If the drawings contain a large number of reference signs, it is strongly recommended to attach a separate sheet listing all reference signs and the features denoted by them.

. . .

This page is intentionally blank.

Appendix 3

Symbols

Graphical drawing symbols, as indicated in 37 CFR 1.84(n), may be used for the conventional elements when appropriate. The elements for which such symbols and labeled representations are used must be adequately identified in the specification.

Known devices should be illustrated by symbols which have a universally recognized conventional meaning and are generally accepted in the art, provided no further detail is essential for understanding the subject matter of the claimed invention. Other symbols may be used on condition that they are not likely to be confused with existing conventional symbols, and that they are readily identifiable.

In general, in lieu of a symbol, a conventional element, combination, or circuit may be shown by an appropriately labeled rectangle, square, or circle; abbreviations should not be used unless their meanings are evident and not confusing with the abbreviations used in the suggested symbols. In electrical symbols, an arrow through an element indicates variability thereof; dotted-line connection of arrows indicates ganging thereof; and inherent property (as resistance) may be indicated by showing symbol (for resistor) in dotted lines.

The American National Standards Institute (ANSI) is a private non-profit organization whose numerous publications include some that pertain to graphical symbols. Such publications,for example, *Graphic Symbols for Fluid Power Diagrams*, *IEEE Standard Graphic Symbols for Logic Functions*, *Graphic Symbols for Electrical and Electronics Diagrams*,are considered to be generally acceptable in patent drawings. ANSI headquarters are at 1819 L Street, NW, Suite 600, Washington, DC 20036, with offices at 25 West 43rd Street, New York, NY 10036. The organization's Internet address is *www.ansi.org*.

Although ANSI documents and other published sources may be used as guides during the selection of graphic symbols for patent drawings, the following should be kept in mind:

- The Office will not "approve" any published collection of symbols as a group, because the use and clarity of symbols must be decided on a case-by-case basis.

- Overly specific symbols should be avoided.

- Symbols with unclear meanings should be labeled for clarification.

- It is always necessary for the specification to include a complete description of the subject matter disclosed.

When the material is an important feature of the invention, the symbols shown on Pages A-3-3 through A-3-5 should be used.

KEY

SURFACE	SECTION

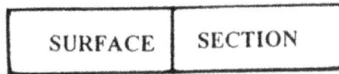

ELEVATION IN SECTION

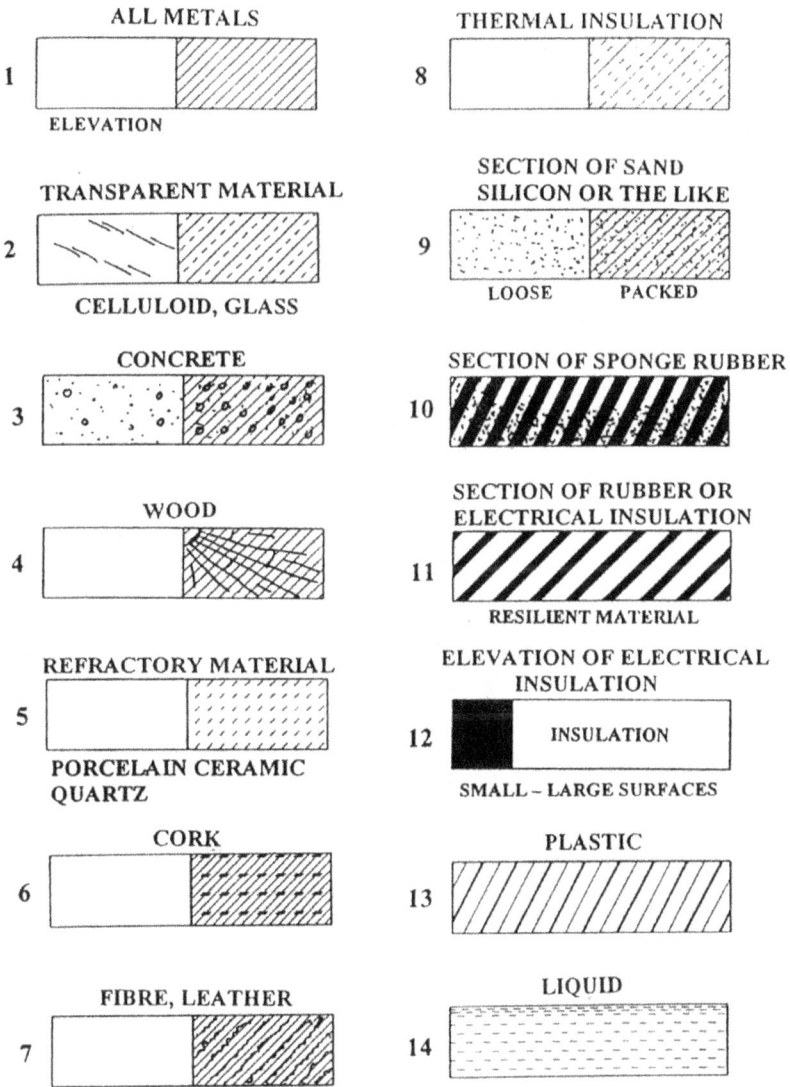

ALL METALS

1

ELEVATION

TRANSPARENT MATERIAL

2

CELLULOID, GLASS

CONCRETE

3

WOOD

4

REFRACTORY MATERIAL

5

PORCELAIN CERAMIC
QUARTZ

CORK

6

FIBRE, LEATHER

7

THERMAL INSULATION

8

**SECTION OF SAND
SILICON OR THE LIKE**

9

LOOSE   PACKED

SECTION OF SPONGE RUBBER

10

**SECTION OF RUBBER OR
ELECTRICAL INSULATION**

11

RESILIENT MATERIAL

**ELEVATION OF ELECTRICAL
INSULATION**

12 INSULATION

SMALL – LARGE SURFACES

PLASTIC

13

LIQUID

14

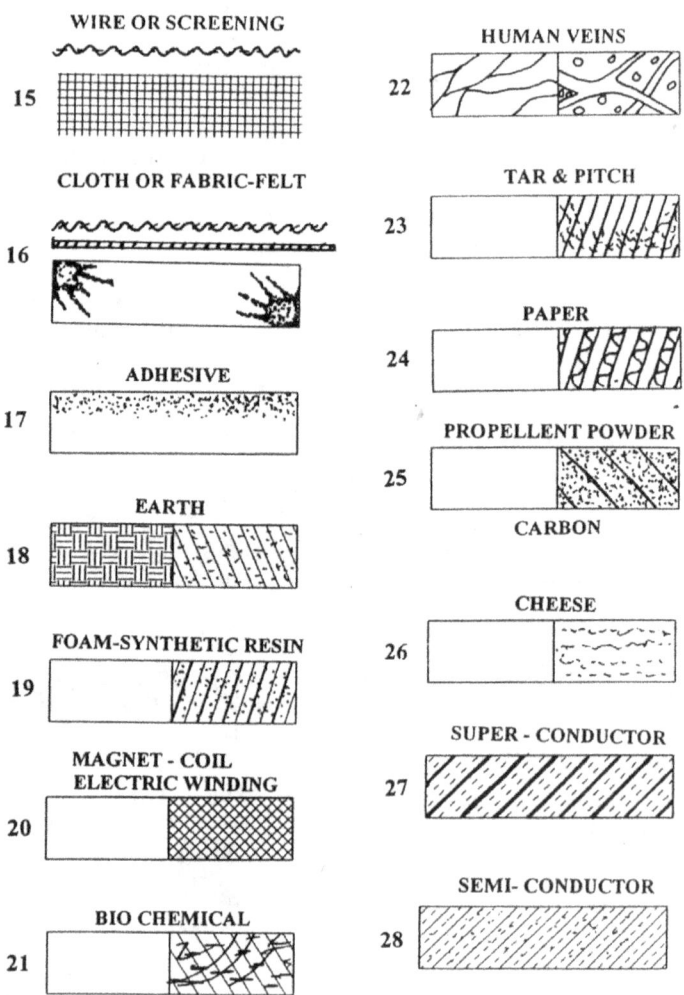

WIRE OR SCREENING

15

CLOTH OR FABRIC-FELT

16

ADHESIVE

17

EARTH

18

FOAM-SYNTHETIC RESIN

19

MAGNET - COIL
ELECTRIC WINDING

20

BIO CHEMICAL

21

HUMAN VEINS

22

TAR & PITCH

23

PAPER

24

PROPELLENT POWDER

25

CARBON

CHEESE

26

SUPER - CONDUCTOR

27

SEMI- CONDUCTOR

28

PACKING ROPE & HEMP

29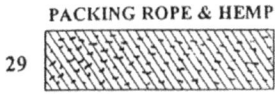

SYNTHETIC SPONGE

30

FRICTION PADS

31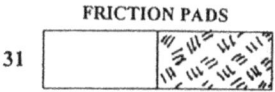

STIPPLE

32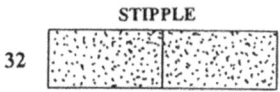

STIPPLE METAL
HATCHING

33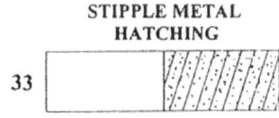

CHEMICAL SOLUTION

34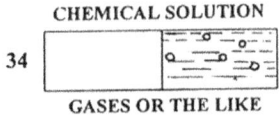

GASES OR THE LIKE

VELCRO®

35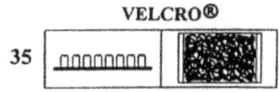

36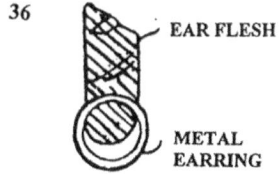

EAR FLESH

METAL
EARRING

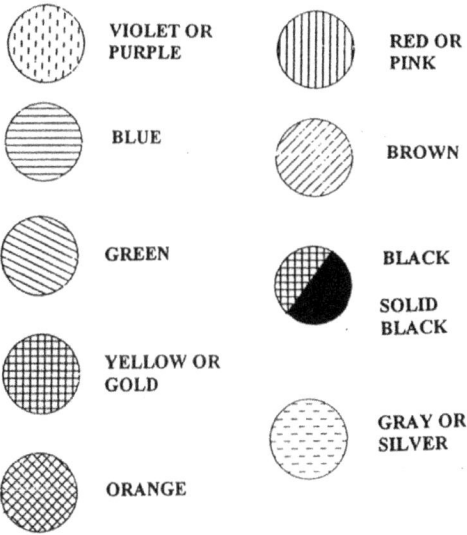

VIOLET OR
PURPLE

BLUE

GREEN

YELLOW OR
GOLD

ORANGE

RED OR
PINK

BROWN

BLACK

SOLID
BLACK

GRAY OR
SILVER

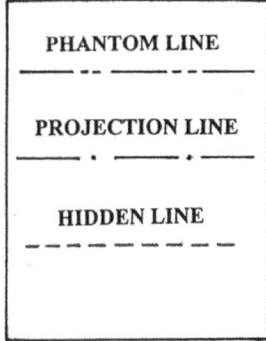

PHANTOM LINE

PROJECTION LINE

HIDDEN LINE

This page is intentionally blank.

Appendix 4

Drawing Examples

Each drawing example in this appendix is intended to focus on one paragraph of 37 CFR 1.84, although each also illustrates other paragraphs of 37 CFR 1.84. The relevant paragraphs are identified on the page facing each example.

It should be kept in mind that an appendix page within which a drawing example appears is not the same as a drawing sheet, so these examples may in some instances depart from a strict conformance to certain paragraphs of 37 CFR 1.84, such as the margin requirements of 37 CFR 1.84(g) and the character-height requirements of 37 CFR 1.84(p)(3).

Sometimes drawings are submitted that include a trademark. Although the use of trademarks is permissible in patent applications, the proprietary nature of the trademarks should be respected and every effort made to prevent their use in any manner, which might adversely affect their validity as trademarks.

This page is intentionally blank.

37 CFR 1.84

NOTE: Because of printing limitations, this guide cannot provide examples of photographic drawings that would be acceptable under 37 CFR 1.84(b).

Example 1

Example 1 is an illustration of a black ink drawing which secures black solid lines in accordance with the requirements of

37 CFR 1.84(a)(1) Black ink.

Additionally, Example 1 illustrates the requirements of

Paragraph (h)(3)	Sectional views. *[hatching]*
Paragraph (i)	Arrangement of views.
Paragraph (l)	Character of lines, numbers, and letters.
Paragraph (m)	Shading.
Paragraph (p)	Numbers, letters, and reference characters.
Paragraph (q)	Lead lines.
Paragraph (r)	Arrows.
Paragraph (u)	Numbering of views.

FIG.1 PRIOR ART

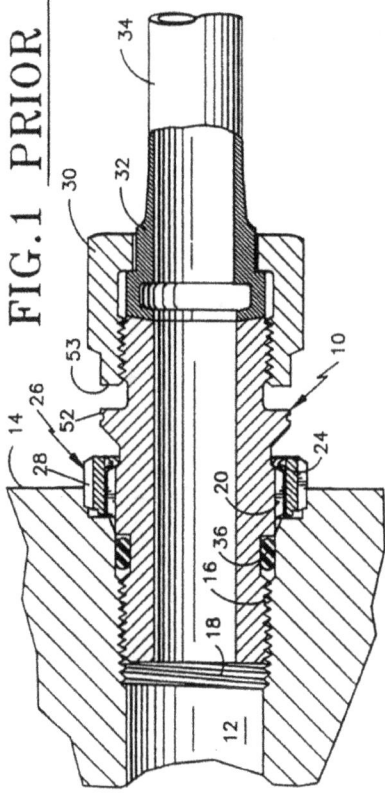

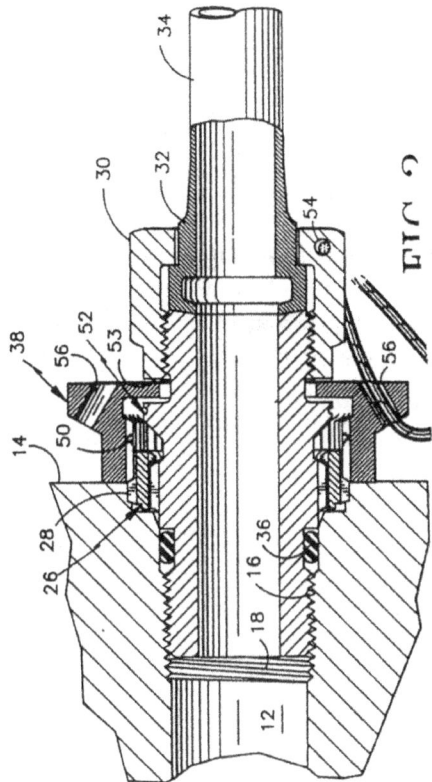

FIG.2

Example 1
Paragraph (a)(1)   Black ink.

Example 2

Example 2 is an illustration which consists of a <u>computer screen image,</u> which is acceptable under the requirements of

37 CFR 1.84(a)(1) Black ink.

A computer screen image, inasmuch as it must show the contents of the screen, is <u>not</u> subject to the "as few words as possible" requirement of Paragraph (o) Legends.

Additionally, Example 2 illustrates the requirements of

Paragraph (i)	Arrangement of views.
Paragraph (l)	Character of lines, numbers, and letters.
Paragraph (p)	Numbers, letters, and reference characters.
Paragraph (u)	Numbering of views.

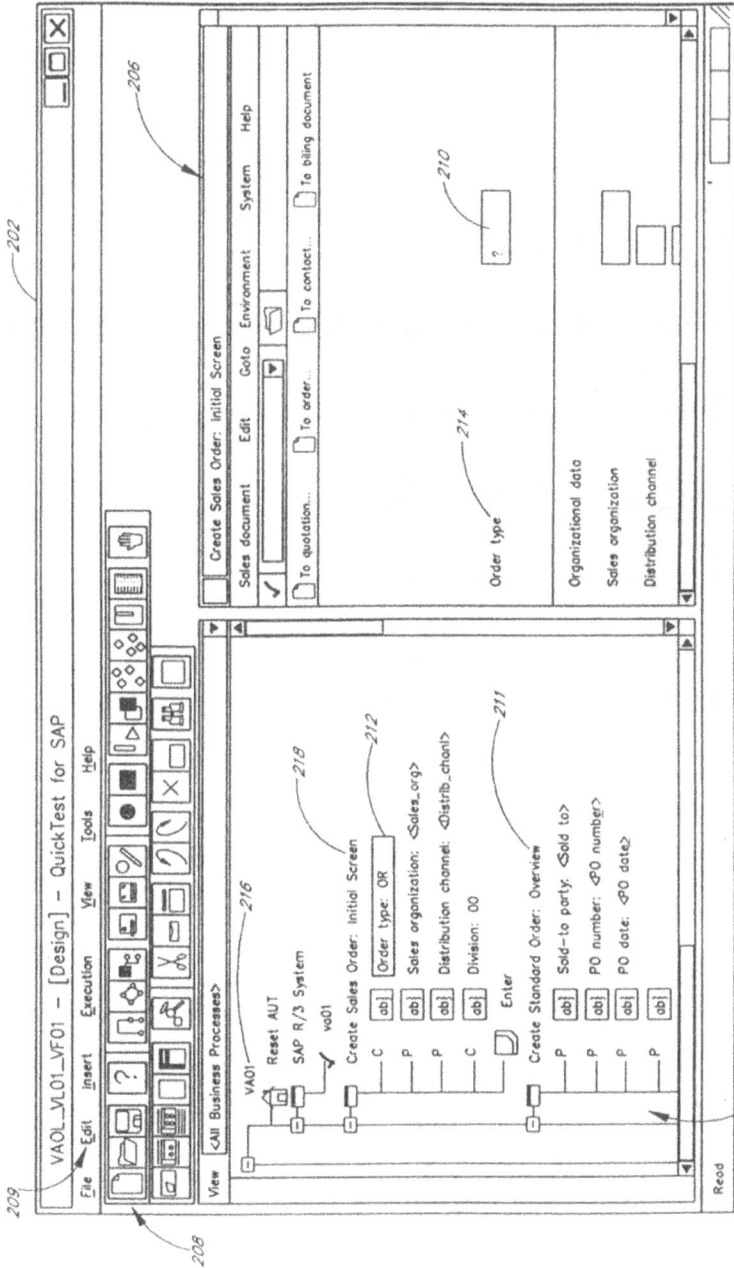

Example 2
37 CFR 1.84 (a)(1) Black ink. *[computer screen image]*

Example 3

Example 3 is an illustration of the proper placement of identifying information (title of invention, inventor's name, application number) on the front of the drawing sheet. This meets the recommendation of

37 CFR 1.84(c) Identification of drawings.

Additionally, Example 3 illustrates the requirements of

Paragraph (a)(1)	Black ink.
Paragraph (g)	Margins.
Paragraph (h)(1)	Exploded views.
Paragraph (l)	Character of lines, numbers, and letters.
Paragraph (m)	Shading.
Paragraph (p)	Numbers, letters, and reference characters.
Paragraph (q)	Lead lines.
Paragraph (r)	Arrows.

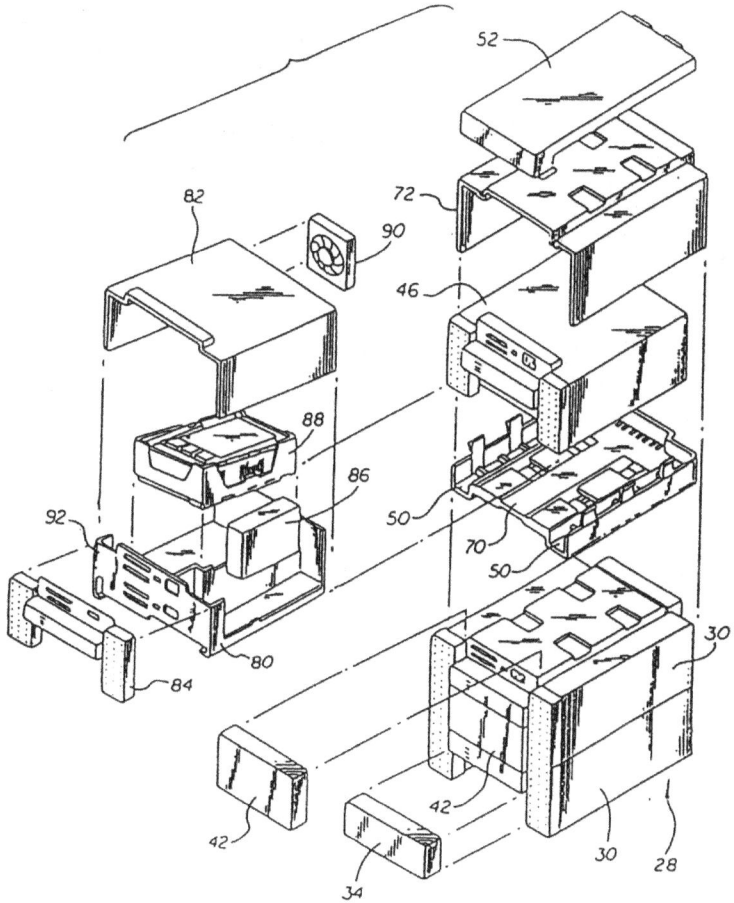

Title of the Invention: Motorcycle Brakes
Inventor's Name: GRAY, Bridget
Docket No./Application No. 09 000,000

Example 3
Paragraph (c)   Identification of drawings. [front of sheet]

Example 4

Example 4 is an illustration of <u>chemical formulae</u>, which may be submitted as drawings. Note that the use of superscript and subscript numerals results in a diminished height where all other numerals meet the requirement of a height of 3.2 mm (Λ inch). This condition is an acceptable exception to the drawing requirements. Otherwise, this illustration meets the requirements of

37 CFR 1.84(d) Graphic forms in drawings.

Additionally, Example 4 illustrates the requirements of

Paragraph (a)(1)	Black ink.
Paragraph (h)	Views.
Paragraph (i)	Arrangement of views.
Paragraph (l)	Character of lines, numbers, and letters.
Paragraph (n)	Symbols.
Paragraph (p)	Numbers, letters, and reference characters.
Paragraph (r)	Arrows.
Paragraph (u)	Numbering of views.

FIG. 4a

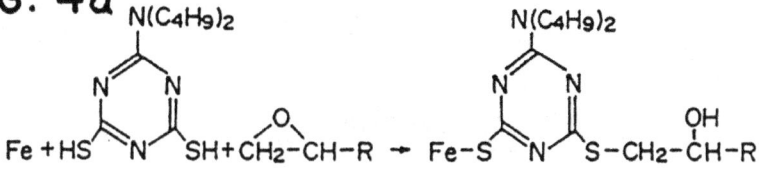

FIG. 4b

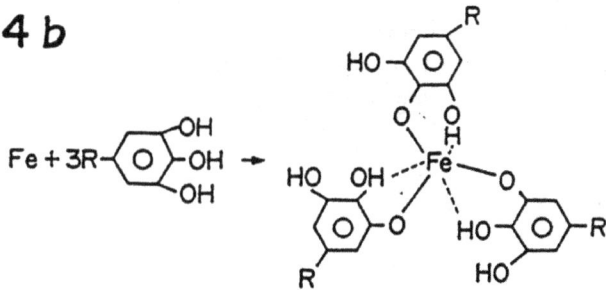

FIG. 4c

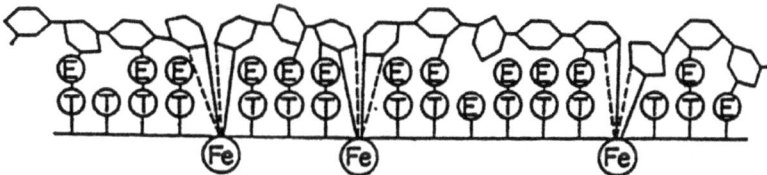

T: Triazine dithiol
E: Epoxy compound

Example 4
Paragraph (d)   Graphic forms in drawings.   *[chemical formulae]*

Example 5

Example 5 is an illustration of <u>waveforms</u>. The drawing meets the requirements of

37 CFR 1.84(d) Graphic forms in drawings.

Additionally, Example 5 illustrates the requirements of

Paragraph (a)(1)	Black ink.
Paragraph (i)	Arrangement of views.
Paragraph (l)	Character of lines, numbers, and letters.
Paragraph (o)	Legends.
Paragraph (p)	Numbers, letters, and reference characters.
Paragraph (q)	Lead lines.
Paragraph (u)	Numbering of views.

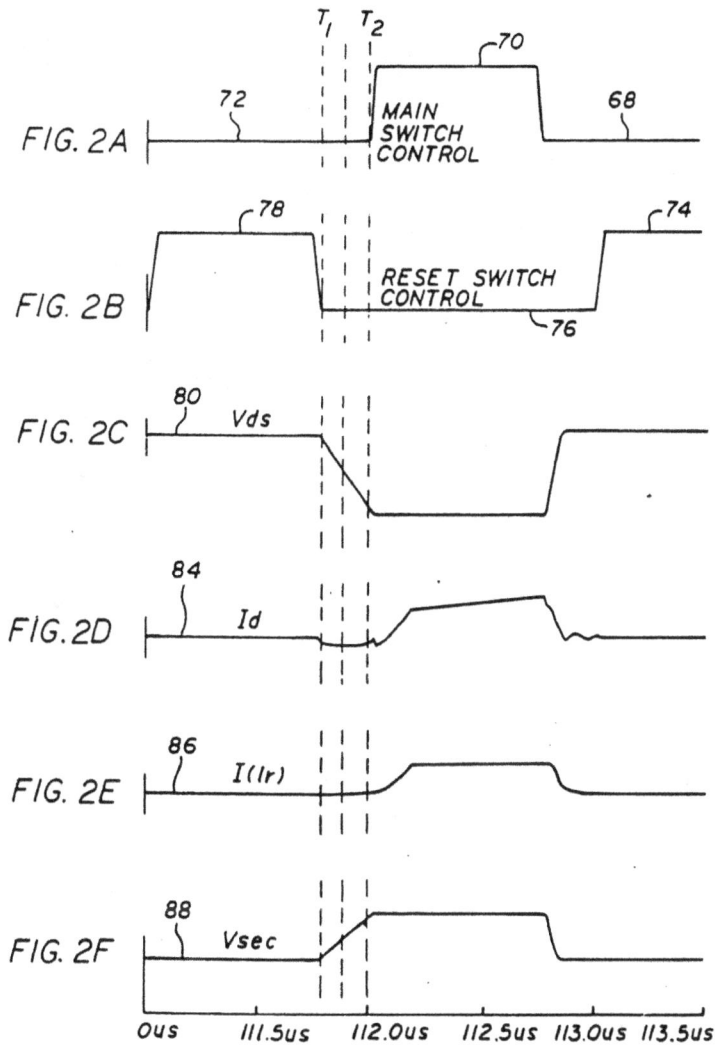

FIG. 2A — 72 — T_1 T_2 — 70 — MAIN SWITCH CONTROL — 68

FIG. 2B — 78 — RESET SWITCH CONTROL — 76 — 74

FIG. 2C — 80 — Vds

FIG.2D — 84 — Id

FIG. 2E — 86 — I(Ir)

FIG. 2F — 88 — Vsec

0us   111.5us   112.0us   112.5us   113.0us   113.5us

Example 5
Paragraph (d)   Graphic forms in drawings. [waveforms]

Example 6

Example 6 is an illustration of a graphical form, which has been used to indicate DNA structure.   The illustration is a representation of an approximation of a section along a DNA molecule. Since a determination cannot be made as to exactly what the structure would look like, the Office allows this approximation to show the believed structure represented. The drawing meets the requirements of

37 CFR 1.84(d) Graphic forms in drawings.

Additionally, Example 6 illustrates the requirements of

Paragraph (a)(1)	Black ink.
Paragraph (i)	Arrangement of views.
Paragraph (l)	Character of lines, numbers, and letters.
Paragraph (n)	Symbols.
Paragraph (o)	Legends.
Paragraph (p)(1)	Numbers, letters, and reference characters.
Paragraph (q)	Lead lines.
Paragraph (r)(1)	Arrows.
Paragraph (u)	Numbering of views.

Example 6 is, however, an **exception** to Paragraph (h)(3), [Sectional views.], in that hatching schemes are used to differentiate the regions of ribonucleic acid (RNA) / deoxyribonucleic acid (DNA). Such schemes are not to be confused with conventional hatching schemes that are used to indicate "proper material(s)."

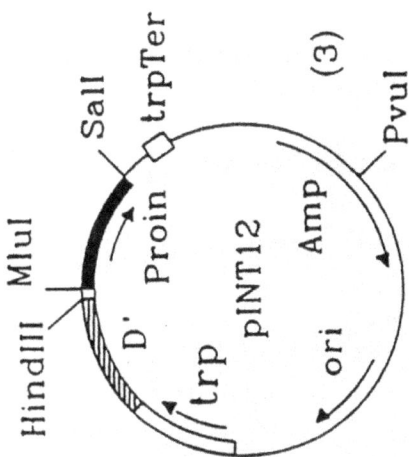

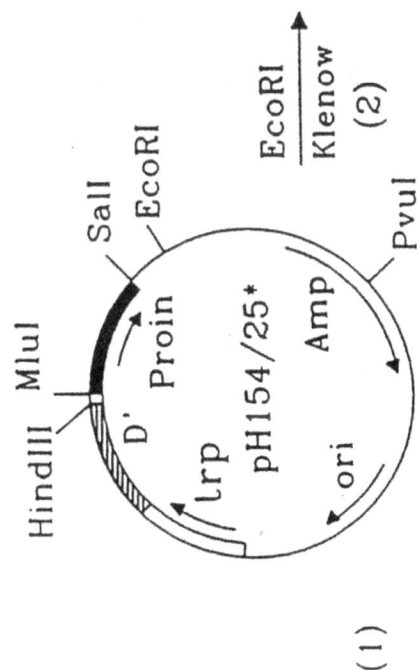

FIG. 1

Example 6
Paragraph (d)   Graphic forms in drawings. *[DNA structures]*

Example 7

Example 7 is an illustration of a design invention, which is presented, in separate views.

37 CFR 1.84(h) Views.

Additionally, Example 7 illustrates the requirements of

Paragraph (a)(1)	Black ink.
Paragraph (i)	Arrangement of views.
Paragraph (l)	Character of lines, numbers, and letters.
Paragraph (m)	Shading.
Paragraph (u)	Numbering of views.

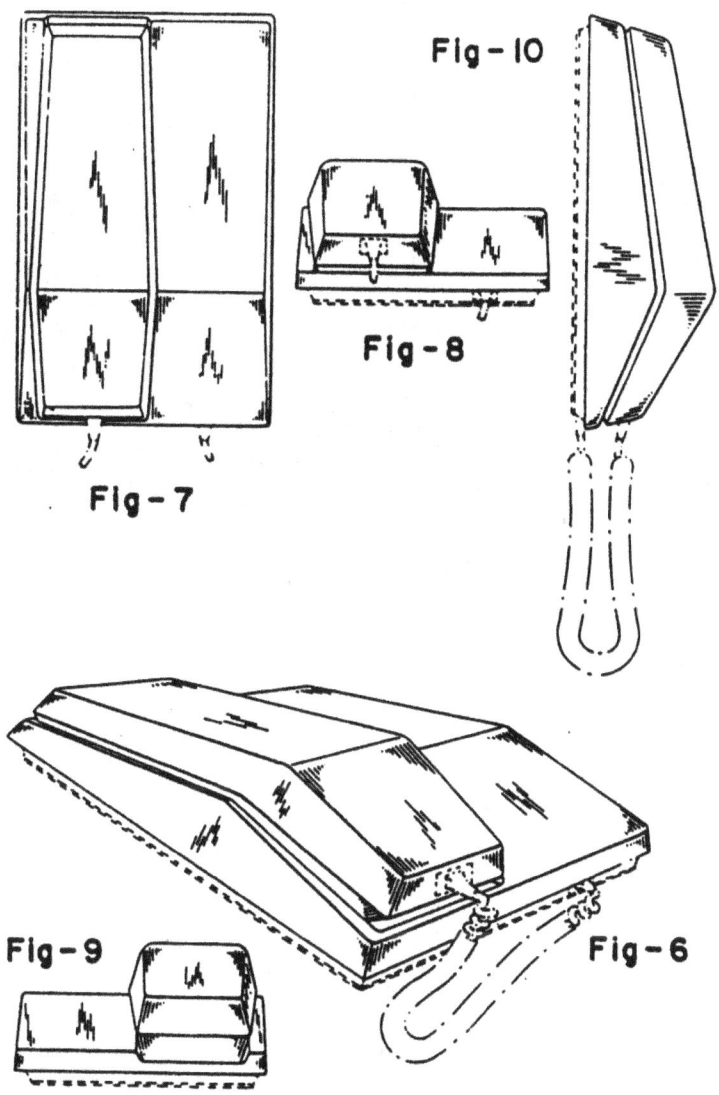

Fig-10

Fig-8

Fig-7

Fig-9

Fig-6

Example 7
Paragraph (h)   Views.

Example 8

Example 8 is an illustration of an exploded view. Although brackets are not required, the example illustrates the proper use of a bracket to delineate the exploded view. The drawing meets the requirements of

37 CFR 1.84(h)(1) Exploded views.

Additionally, Example 8 illustrates the requirements of

Paragraph (a)(1)	Black ink.
Paragraph (i)	Arrangement of views.
Paragraph (l)	Character of lines, numbers, and letters.
Paragraph (p)(1)	Numbers, letters, and reference characters.
Paragraph (q)	Lead lines.
Paragraph (r)(1)	Arrows.
Paragraph (u)	Numbering of views.

FIG.2

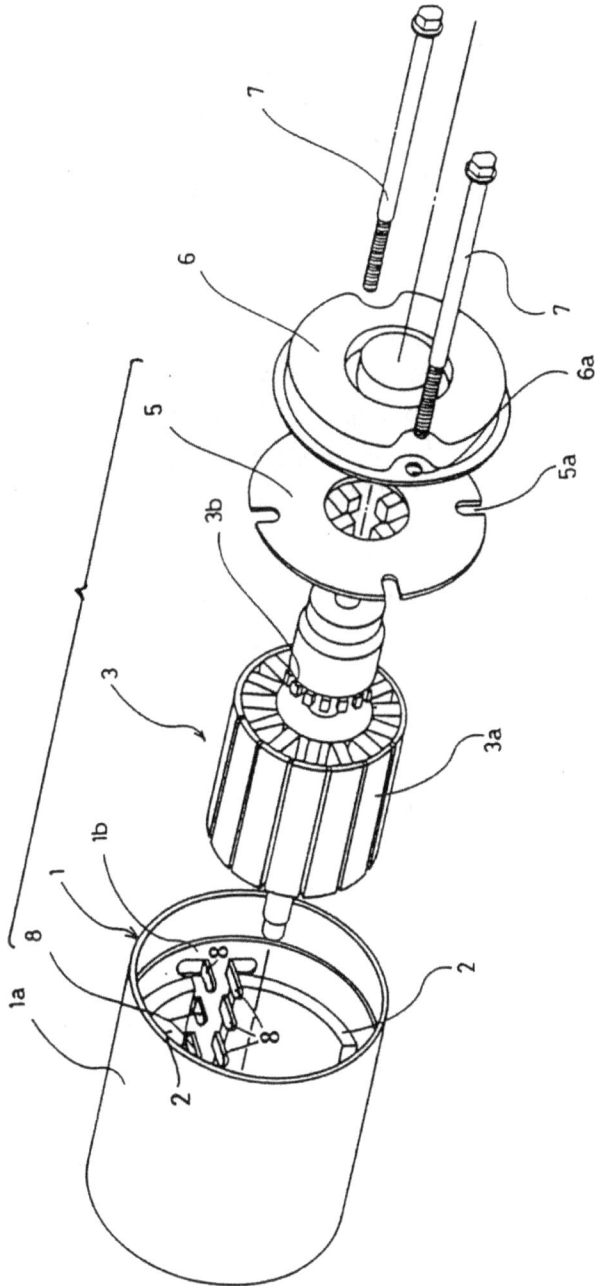

Example 8
Paragraph (h)(1)   Exploded views.

Example 9

Example 9 is an illustration of partial views. FIG. 8 is "a portion of a view ... enlarged for magnification purposes." Note that each figure is labeled separately. The drawing meets the requirements of

37 CFR 1.84(h)(2) Partial views.

Additionally, Example 9 illustrates the requirements of

Paragraph (a)(1)	Black ink.
Paragraph (h)(3)	Sectional views. *[hatching]*
Paragraph (i)	Arrangement of views.
Paragraph (l)	Character of lines, numbers, and letters.
Paragraph (p)	Numbers, letters, and reference characters.
Paragraph (q)	Lead lines.
Paragraph (r)(1)	Arrows.
Paragraph (u)	Numbering of views.

FIG. 7

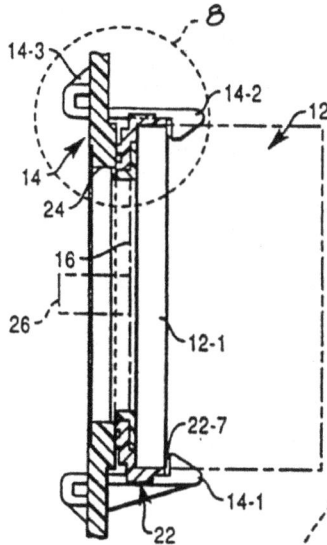

FIG. 8

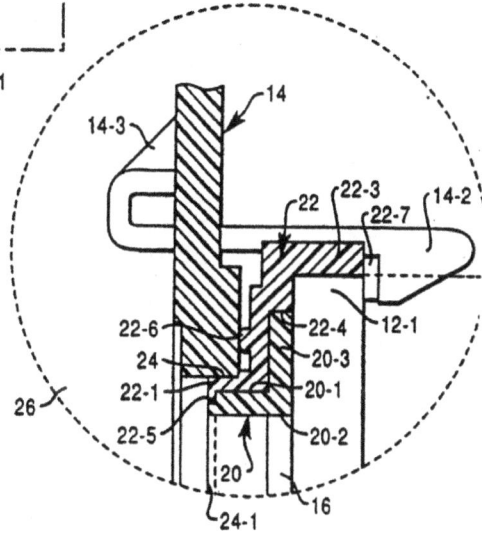

Example 9
Paragraph (h)(2) Partial views.

Example 10

Example 10 is an illustration of a sectional view. Figure 2 is a section of the object depicted in Figure 1. Note that the plane upon which Figure 2 is taken is indicated in Figure 1 by the broken lines 2 + + 2, and that arrows are used in Figure 1 as indications of the direction of sight. The drawing meets the requirements of

37 CFR 1.84(h)(3) Sectional views.

Additionally, Example 10 illustrates the requirements of

Paragraph (a)(1)	Black ink.
Paragraph (h)	Views.
Paragraph (i)	Arrangement of views.
Paragraph (l)	Character of lines, numbers, and letters.
Paragraph (m)	Shading.
Paragraph (p)	Numbers, letters, and reference characters.
Paragraph (q)	Lead lines.
Paragraph (r)	Arrows.
Paragraph (u)	Numbering of views.

Much of Paragraph (h)(3) pertains to the technique of hatching. However, most of the spaced lines in Example 10 are examples of the technique of shading, as described in Paragraph (m). For examples of hatching as described in Paragraph (h)(3), see Examples 1, 9, 11, 12, 14, 15, 20, 21, and 25.

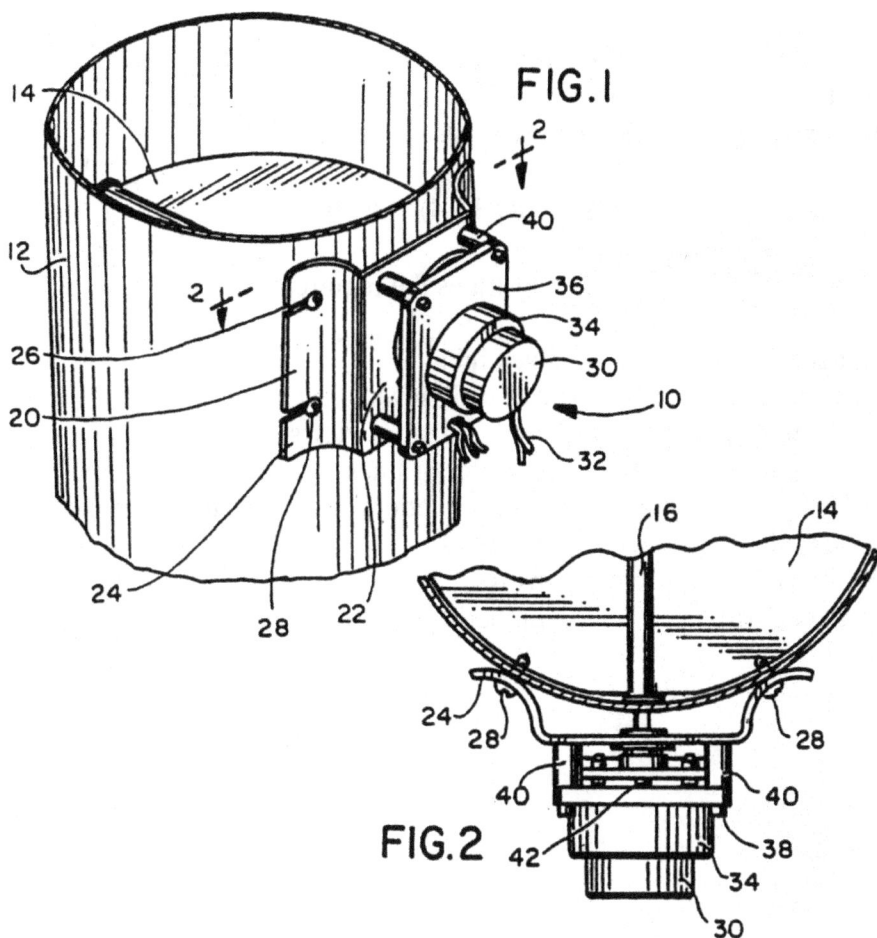

FIG.1

FIG.2

Example 10
Paragraph (h)(3)   Sectional views.

Example 11

Example 11 is an illustration of a drawing which contains an alternate position. Note that the cover is shown by broken lines in a raised position. The drawing meets the requirements of

37 CFR 1.84(h)(4) Alternate position.

Additionally, Example 11 illustrates the requirements of

Paragraph (a)(1)	Black ink.
Paragraph (h)(3)	Sectional views. *[hatching]*
Paragraph (i)	Arrangement of views.
Paragraph (l)	Character of lines, numbers, and letters.
Paragraph (p)	Numbers, letters, and reference characters.
Paragraph (q)	Lead lines.
Paragraph (r)	Arrows.
Paragraph (u)	Numbering of views.

FIG. 9

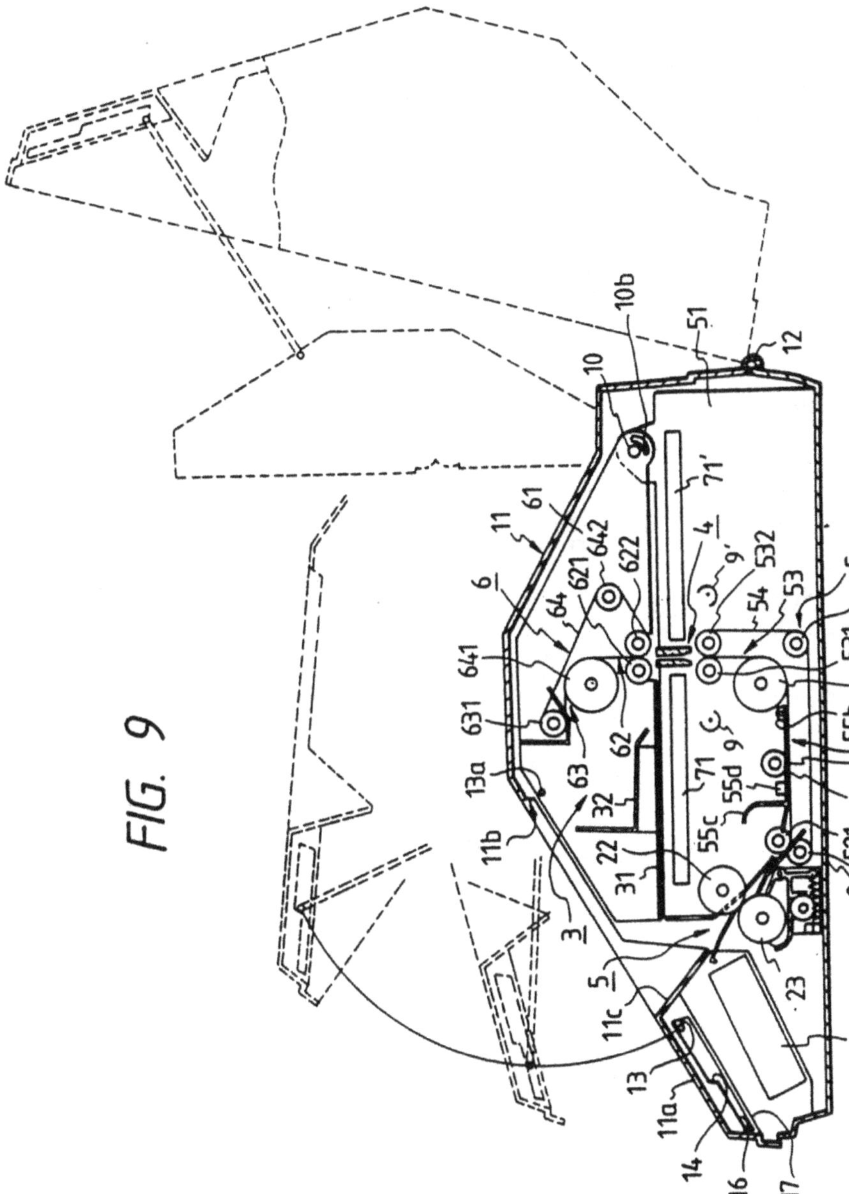

Example 11

Paragraph (h)(4)   Alternate position.

Example 12

Example 12 is an illustration of a drawing, which contains modified forms. Note that FIG. 1 shows fastening means 52 and 53, and FIG. 2 shows fastening means 62 and 63. The drawing meets the requirements of

37 CFR 1.84(h)(5) Modified forms.

Additionally, Example 12 illustrates the requirements of

Paragraph (a)(1)	Black ink.
Paragraph (h)(3)	Sectional views. *[hatching]*
Paragraph (i)	Arrangement of views.
Paragraph (l)	Character of lines, numbers, and letters.
Paragraph (m)	Shading.
Paragraph (p)	Numbers, letters, and reference characters.
Paragraph (q)	Lead lines.
Paragraph (u)	Numbering of views.

FIG. 2

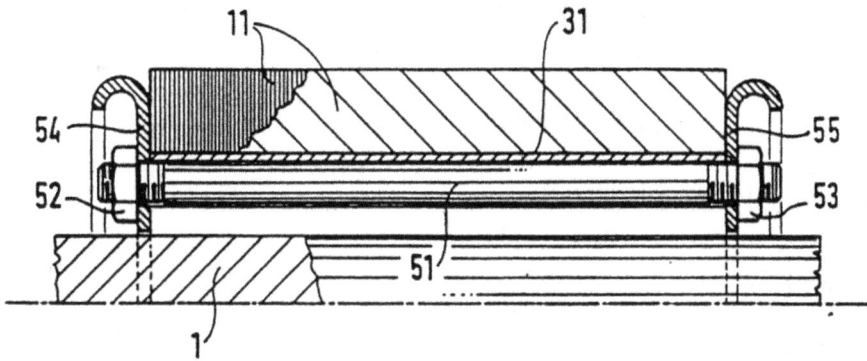

FIG. 3

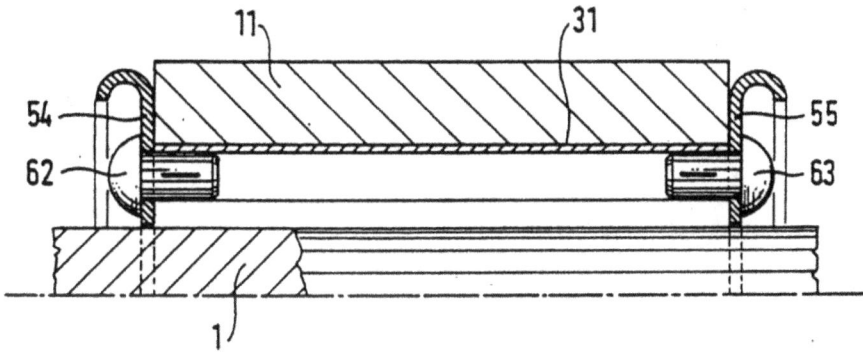

Example 12
Paragraph (h)(5)   Modified forms.

Example 13

Example 13 illustrates how views should stand on a sheet so that "Words ... appear in a horizontal, left-to-right fashion when the page is either upright or turned so that the top becomes the right side." This example illustrates

37 CFR 1.84(i) Arrangement of views.

Additionally, Example 13 illustrates the requirements of

Paragraph (a)(1)	Black ink.
Paragraph (l)	Character of lines, numbers, and letters.
Paragraph (o)	Legends.

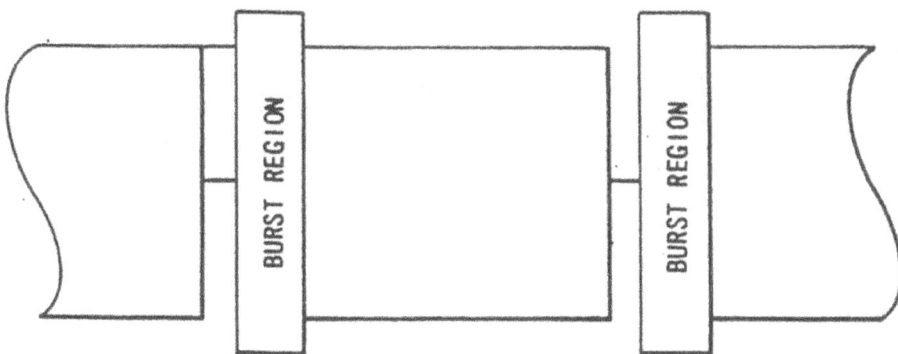

BURST REGION

BURST REGION

Example 13
Paragraph (i)   Arrangement of views.

Example 14

Example 14 is an illustration of a view that includes the overall organization of the device to provide a view for suitable for publication on the front page of the patent application publication and the front page of the patent. The drawing meets the requirements of

37 CFR 1.84(j) Front page view.

Additionally, Example 14 illustrates the requirements of

Paragraph (a)(1)   Black ink.
Paragraph (h)(3)   Sectional views. *[hatching]*
Paragraph (i)   Arrangement of views.
Paragraph (l)   Character of lines, numbers, and letters.
Paragraph (p)   Numbers, letters, and reference characters.
Paragraph (q)   Lead lines.
Paragraph (u)   Numbering of views.

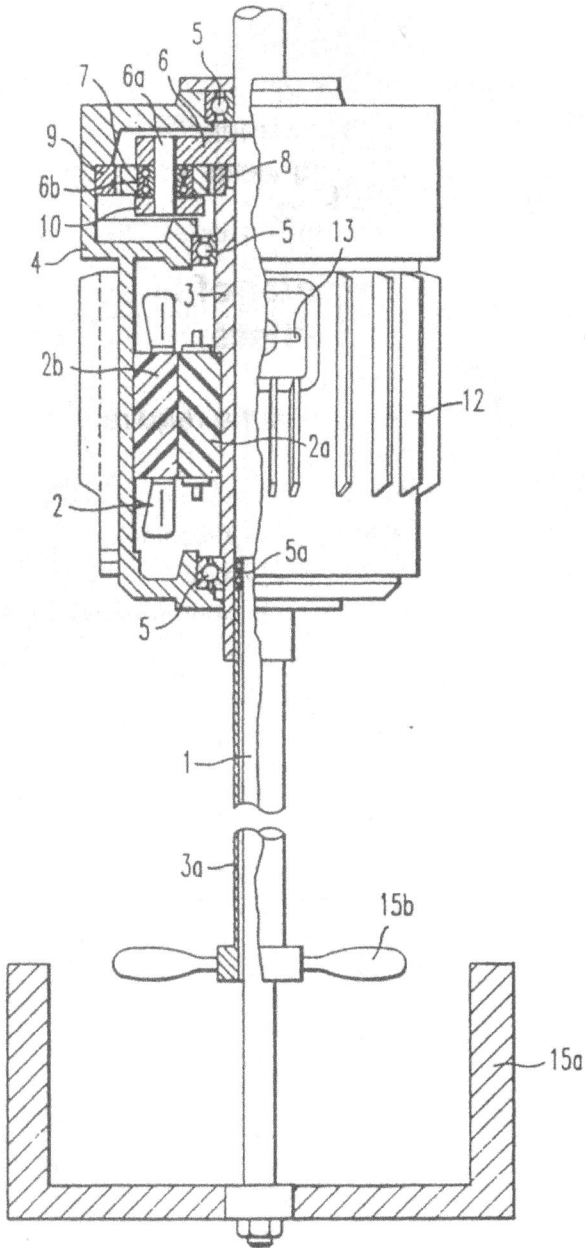

FIG. 2

Example 14
37 CFR 1.84 (j) Front page view.

Example 15

Example 15 is an illustration of the character of lines and numbers in a drawing. The example illustrates a continuous thick line for edging and outlining views and cross-sections. The drawing meets the requirements of

37 CFR 1.84(l) Character of lines, numbers, and letters.

Additionally, Example 15 illustrates the requirements of

Paragraph (a)(1)	Black ink.
Paragraph (h)(3)	Sectional views. *[hatching]*
Paragraph (i)	Arrangement of views.
Paragraph (p)	Numbers, letters, and reference characters.
Paragraph (q)	Lead lines.
Paragraph (u)	Numbering of views.

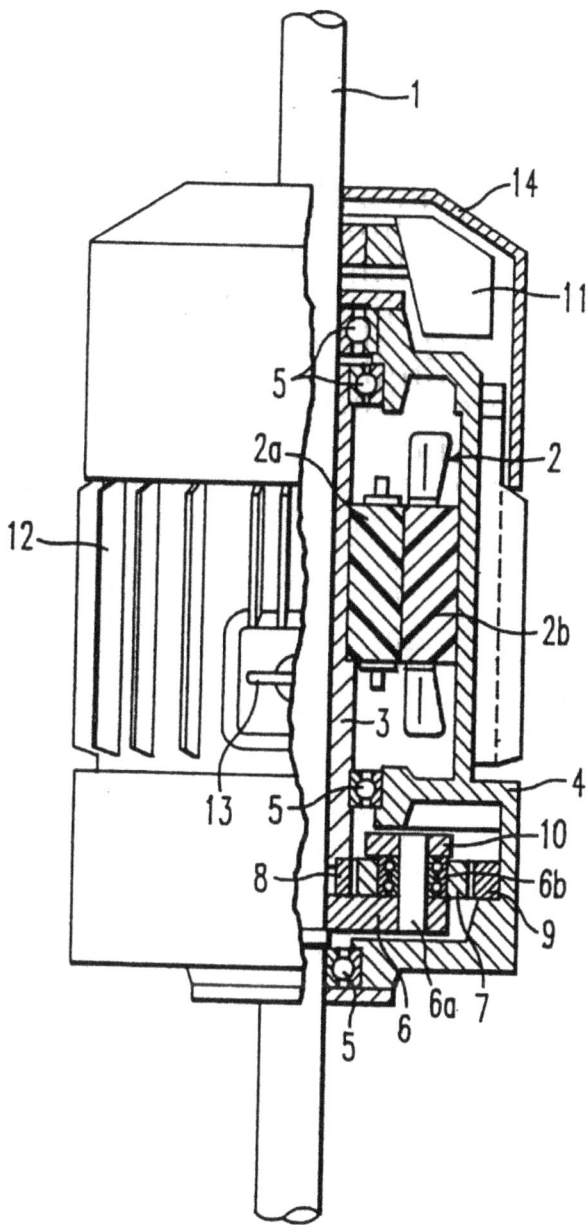

FIG. 1

Example 15
Paragraph (I)   Character of lines, numbers, and letters.

Example 16

Example 16 illustrates the use of <u>spaced lines</u> as acceptable shading for opaque surfaces. This drawing meets the requirements of

37 CFR 1.84(m) Shading.

Additionally, Example 16 illustrates the requirements of

Paragraph (a)(1)	Black ink.
Paragraph (i)	Arrangement of views.
Paragraph (u)	Numbering of views.

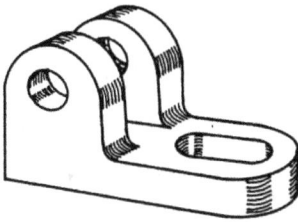

Figure 1

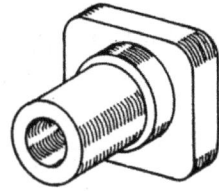

Figure 2

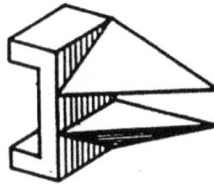

Figure 3

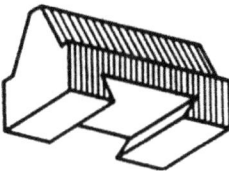

Figure 4

Example 16
Paragraph (m)   Shading.   *[spaced lines]*

Example 17

Example 17 illustrates the use of <u>stippling</u> as acceptable shading for opaque surfaces. The drawing meets the requirements of

37 CFR 1.84(m) Shading.

Additionally, Example 17 illustrates the requirements of

Paragraph (a)(1)   Black ink.
Paragraph (l)   Character of lines, numbers, and letters.

FIG-1

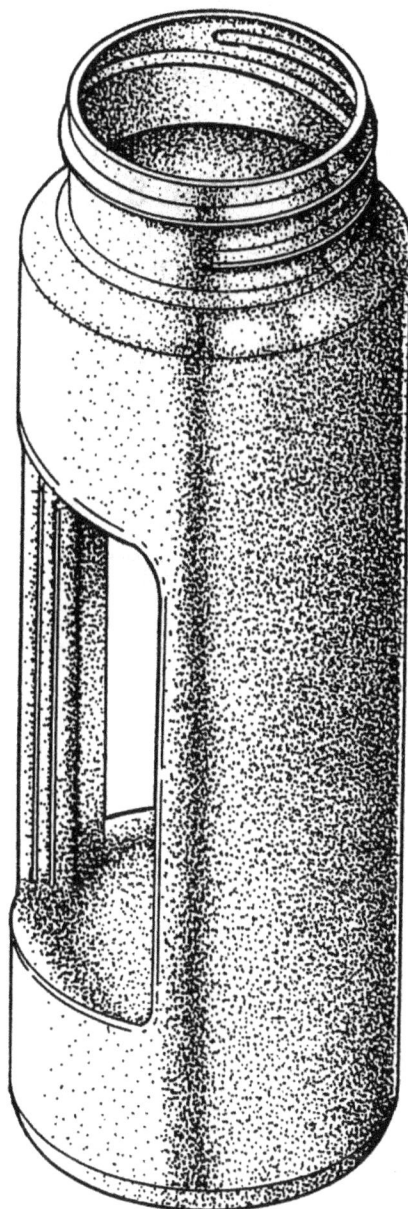

Example 17
Paragraph (m) Shading. *[stippling]*

Example 18

Example 18 illustrates the use of acceptable symbols—in this instance, the use of common electrical symbols. The drawing meets the requirements of

37 CFR 1.84(n) Symbols.

Additionally, Example 18 illustrates the requirements of

Paragraph (a)(1)	Black ink.
Paragraph (i)	Arrangement of views.
Paragraph (l)	Character of lines, numbers, and letters.
Paragraph (p)	Numbers, letters, and reference characters.
Paragraph (q)	Lead lines.
Paragraph (r)	Arrows.
Paragraph (u)	Numbering of views.

Fig. 5

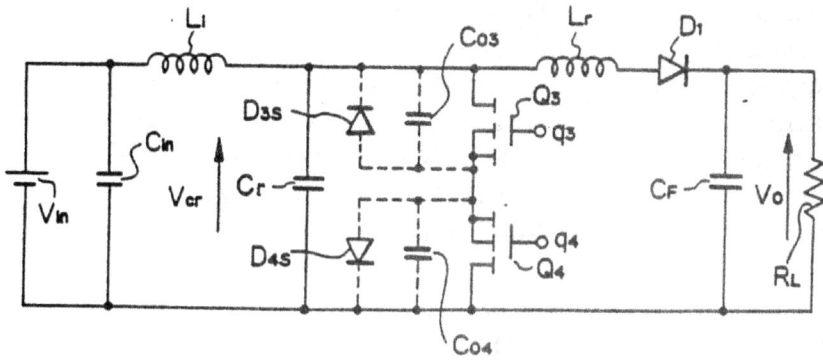

Example 18
Paragraph (n) Symbols.

Example 19

Example 19 illustrates the use of acceptable descriptive legends. The drawing meets the requirements of

37 CFR 1.84(o) Legends.

Additionally, Example 19 illustrates the requirements of

Paragraph (a)(1)	Black ink.
Paragraph (i)	Arrangement of views.
Paragraph (l)	Character of lines, numbers, and letters.
Paragraph (p)	Numbers, letters, and reference characters.
Paragraph (q)	Lead lines.
Paragraph (r)	Arrows.
Paragraph (u)	Numbering of views.

See Example 2. Computer screen images are not subject to the "as few words as possible" requirement of Paragraph (o).

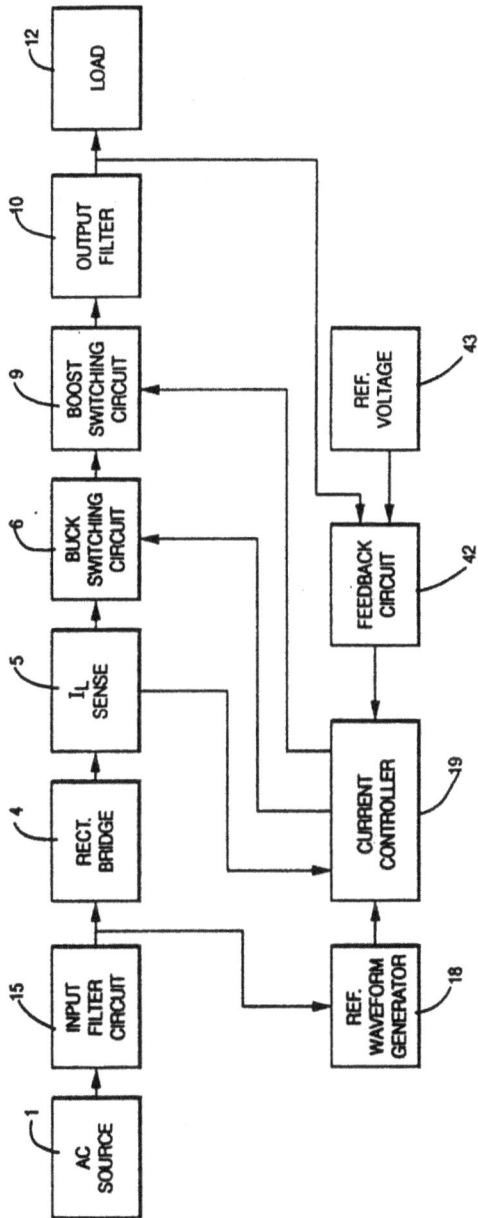

FIG. 3

Example **19**
Paragraph (o)   Legends.

Example 20

Example 20 meets the requirements of

37 CFR 1.84(p) Numbers, letters, and reference characters.

Additionally, Example 20 illustrates the requirements of

Paragraph (a)(1)	Black ink.
Paragraph (h)(3)	Sectional views. *[hatching]*
Paragraph (l)	Character of lines, numbers, and letters.
Paragraph (q)	Lead lines.
Paragraph (r)	Arrows.

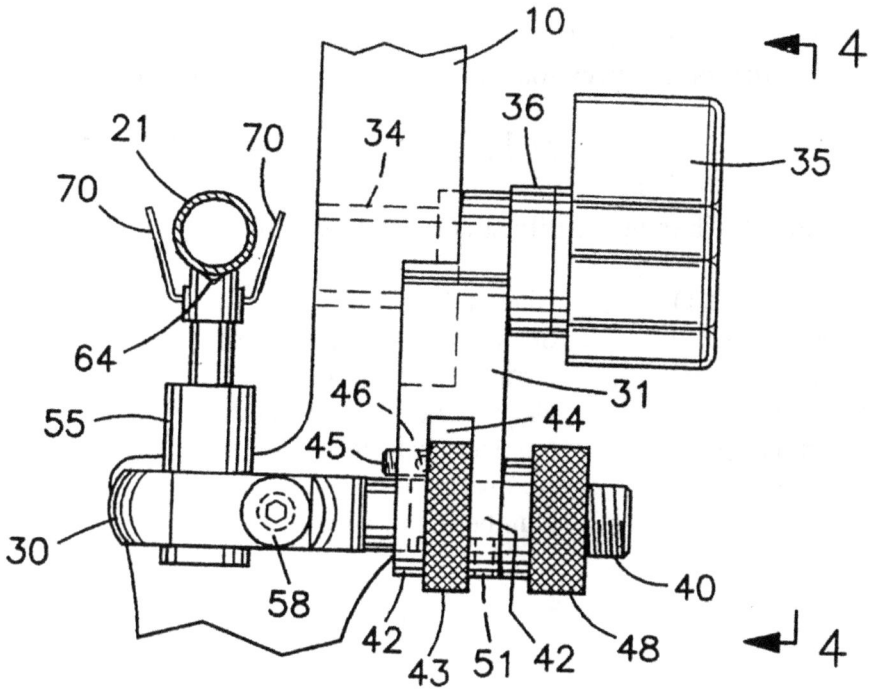

Example 20
Paragraph (p)   Numbers, letters, and reference characters.

Example 21

Example 21 illustrates the use of lead lines to match reference characters to the structure of the invention. The drawing meets the requirements of

37 CFR 1.84(q) Lead lines.

Additionally, Example 21 illustrates the requirements of

Paragraph (a)(1)	Black ink.
Paragraph (h)(3)	Sectional views. *[hatching]*
Paragraph (i)	Arrangement of views.
Paragraph (l)	Character of lines, numbers, and letters.
Paragraph (p)	Numbers, letters, and reference characters.
Paragraph (r)	Arrows.
Paragraph (u)	Numbering of views.

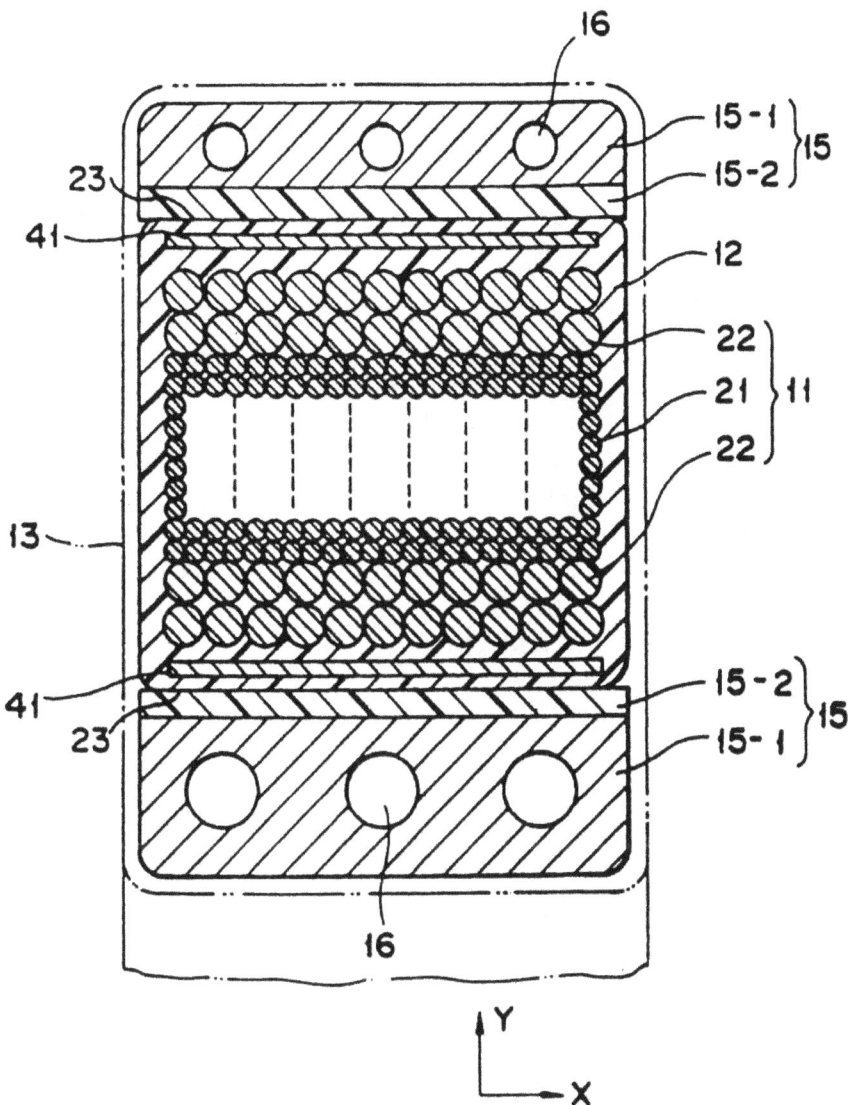

F I G. 6

Example 21
Paragraph (q)   Lead lines.

Example 22

Example 22 illustrates the use of arrows. Note that some arrows (20, 21) indicate a structural area while other arrows (4', 21') indicate a direction of motion or rotation. The drawing meets the requirements of

37 CFR 1.84(r) Arrows.

Additionally, Example 22 illustrates the requirements of

Paragraph (a)(1)	Black ink.
Paragraph (i)	Arrangement of views.
Paragraph (l)	Character of lines, numbers, and letters.
Paragraph (m)	Shading.
Paragraph (n)	Symbols.
Paragraph (p)	Numbers, letters, and reference characters.
Paragraph (q)	Lead lines.
Paragraph (u)	Numbering of views.

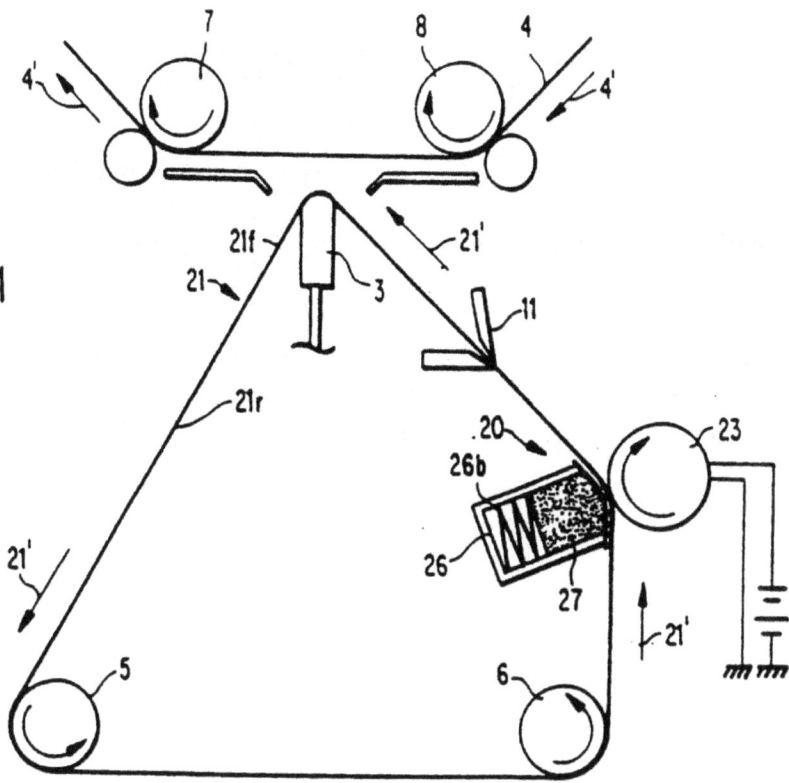

FIG. 1

Example 22
Paragraph (r)   Arrows.

Example 23

Example 23 illustrates the presence of a copyright notice on a drawing. The drawing meets the requirements of

37 CFR 1.84(s) Copyright or Mask Work Notice.

Additionally, Example 23 illustrates the requirements of

Paragraph (a)(1)	lack ink.
Paragraph (i)	Arrangement of views.
Paragraph (l)	Character of lines, number, and letters.
Paragraph (m)	Shading.

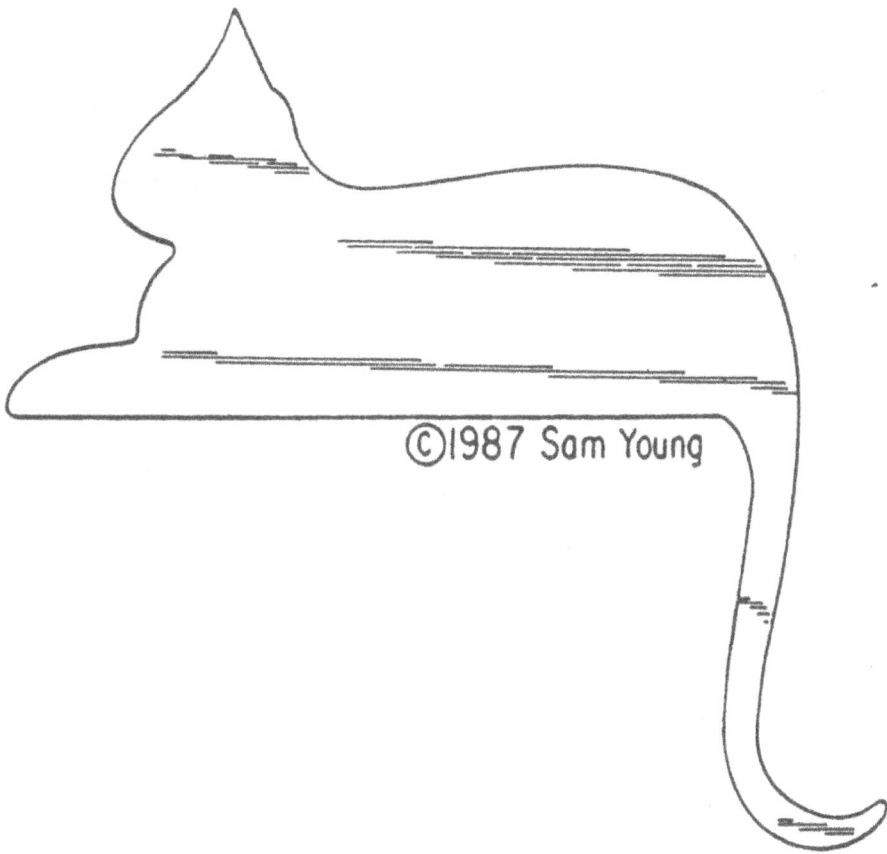

©1987 Sam Young

Example 23
Paragraph (s)   Copyright or Mask Work Notice.

Example 24

Example 24 illustrates correct numbering of a drawing sheet. The drawing meets the requirements of

37 CFR 1.84(t) Numbering of sheets of drawings.

Additionally, Example 24 illustrates the requirements of

Paragraph (a)(1)	Black ink.
Paragraph (h)(1)	Exploded views.
Paragraph (i)	Arrangement of views.
Paragraph (l)	Character of lines, numbers, and letters.
Paragraph (p)	Numbers, letters, and reference characters.
Paragraph (q)	Lead lines.
Paragraph (r)	Arrows.
Paragraph (u)	Numbering of views.

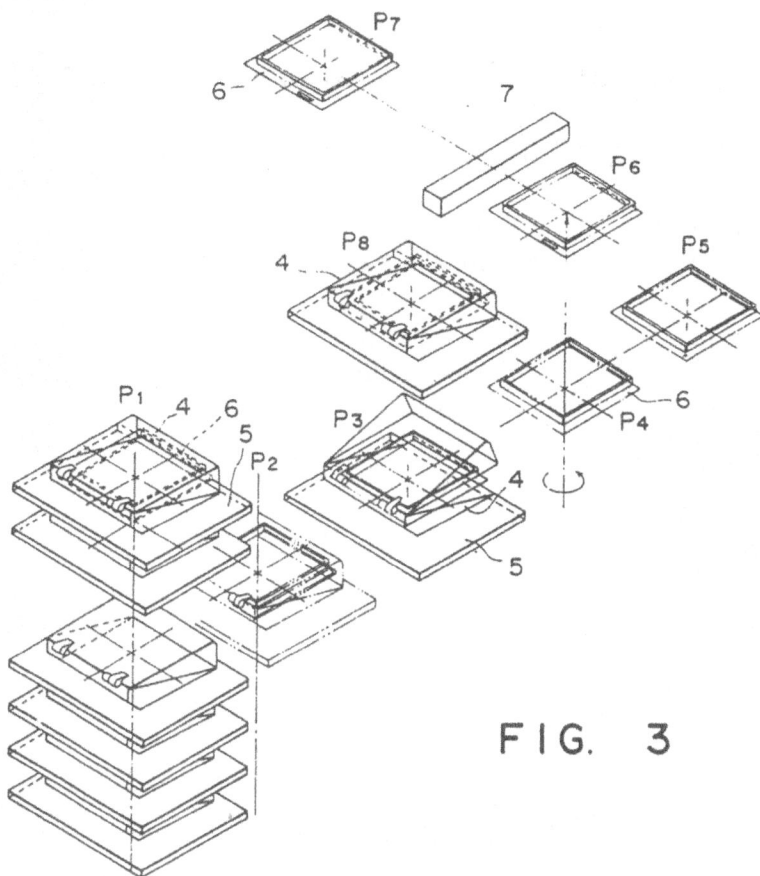

FIG. 3

Example 24
Paragraph (t)   Numbering of sheets of drawings.

Example 25

Example 25 illustrates the correct numbering of views. The drawing meets the requirements of

37 CFR 1.84(u) Numbering of views.

Additionally, Example 25 illustrates the requirements of

Paragraph (a)(1)	Black ink.
Paragraph (h)(3)	Sectional views. *[hatching]*
Paragraph (i)	Arrangement of views.
Paragraph (l)	Character of lines, numbers, and letters.
Paragraph (p)	Numbers, letters, and reference characters.
Paragraph (q)	Lead lines.

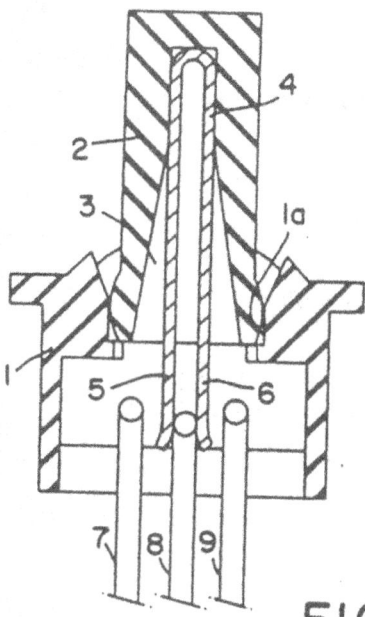

FIG. I

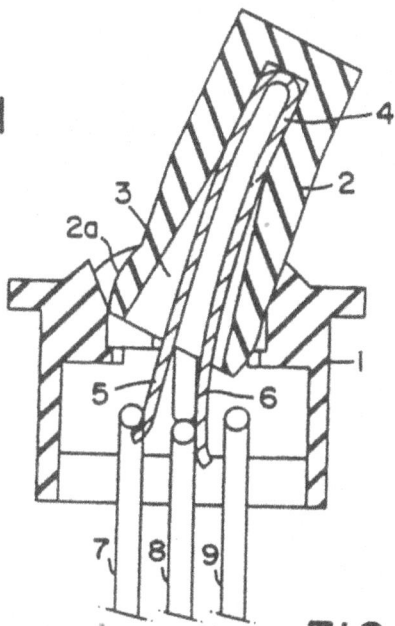

FIG. 2

Example 25
Paragraph (u)   Numbering of views.

This page is intentionally blank.

Appendix 5

Form PTO-948 (Rev. 04/02)

Form PTO-948, Notice of Draftsperson's Patent Drawing Review, is used by the Office to indicate its disapproval of submitted drawings.

When drawings are objected to by the Office draftsperson under 37 CFR 1.84 or 1.152, the draftsperson uses the boxed section of Form PTO-948 to identify the informalities (deficiencies). The boxed section of the form reflects the sequence of the paragraphs of 37 CFR 1.84 and has been designed so that the Office draftsperson can indicate each possible drafting error.

The completed Form PTO-948 is held for mailing with the next Office action.

See Pages 3 and 4 of this guide.

This page is intentionally blank.

Form PTO 948 (Rev. 04/02)   U.S. DEPARTMENT OF COMMERCE - Patent and Trademark Office   Application No._____

NOTICE OF DRAFTSPERSON'S
PATENT DRAWING REVIEW

The drawing(s) filed (insert date)_____ are:
A. ☐ approved by the Draftsperson under 37 CFR 1.84 or 1.152.
B. ☐ objected to by the Draftsperson under 37 CFR 1.84 or 1.152 for the reasons indicated below. The Examiner will require submission of new, corrected drawings when necessary. Corrected drawing must be sumitted according to the instructions on the back of this notice.

1. DRAWINGS. 37 CFR 1.84(a): Acceptable categories of drawings:
   Black ink. Color.
   ____ Color drawings are not acceptable until petition is granted.
   Fig(s) _____
   ____ Pencil and non black ink not permitted. Fig(s) _____
2. PHOTOGRAPHS. 37 CFR 1.84(b)
   ____ 1 full-tone set is required. Fig(s) _____
   ____ Photographs may not be mounted. 37 CFR 1.84(e)
   ____ Poor quality (half-tone). Fig(s) _____
3. TYPE OF PAPER. 37 CFR 1.84(e)
   ____ Paper not flexible, strong, white, and durable.
   Fig(s) _____
   ____ Erasures, alterations, overwritings, interlineations,
   folds, copy machine marks not accepted. Fig(s) _____
   ____ Mylar, velum paper is not acceptable (too thin).
   Fig(s) _____
4. SIZE OF PAPER. 37 CFR 1.84(f): Acceptable sizes:
   ____ 21.0 cm by 29.7 cm (DIN size A4)
   ____ 21.6 cm by 27.9 cm (8 1/2 x 11 inches)
   ____ All drawing sheets not the same size.
   Sheet(s) _____
   ____ Drawings sheets not an acceptable size. Fig(s) _____
5. MARGINS. 37 CFR 1.84(g): Acceptable margins:

   Top 2.5 cm Left 2.5cm Right 1.5 cm Bottom 1.0 cm
   SIZE: A4 Size
   Top 2.5 cm Left 2.5 cm Right 1.5 cm Bottom 1.0 cm
   SIZE: 8 1/2 x 11
   Margins not acceptable. Fig(s) _____
   _____ Top (T) _____ Left (L)
   _____ Right (R) _____ Bottom (B)
6. VIEWS. 37 CFR 1.84(h)
   REMINDER: Specification may require revision to
   correspond to drawing changes.
   Partial views. 37 CFR 1.84(h)(2)
   ____ Brackets needed to show figure as one entity.
   Fig(s) _____
   ____ Views not labeled separately or properly.
   Fig(s) _____
   ____ Enlarged view not labeled separetely or properly.
   Fig(s) _____

7. SECTIONAL VIEWS. 37 CFR 1.84 (h)(3)
   ____ Hatching not indicated for sectional portions of an object.
   Fig(s) _____
   ____ Sectional designation should be noted with Arabic or
   Roman numbers. Fig(s) _____

8. ARRANGEMENT OF VIEWS. 37 CFR 1.84(i)
   ____ Words do not appear on a horizontal, left-to-right fashion
   when page is either upright or turned so that the top
   becomes the right side, except for graphs. Fig(s) _____
9. SCALE. 37 CFR 1.84(k)
   ____ Scale not large enough to show mechanism without
   crowding when drawing is reduced in size to two-thirds in
   reproduction.
   Fig(s) _____
10. CHARACTER OF LINES, NUMBERS, & LETTERS.
   37 CFR 1.84(l)
   ____ Lines, numbers & letters not uniformly thick and well
   defined, clean, durable, and black (poor line quality).
   Fig(s) _____
11. SHADING. 37 CFR 1.84(m)
   ____ Solid black areas pale. Fig(s) _____
   ____ Solid black shading not permitted. Fig(s) _____
   ____ Shade lines, pale, rough and blurred. Fig(s) _____
12. NUMBERS, LETTERS, & REFERENCE CHARACTERS.
   37 CFR 1.84(p)
   ____ Numbers and reference characters not plain and legible.
   Fig(s) _____
   ____ Figure legends are poor. Fig(s) _____
   ____ Numbers and reference characters not oriented in the
   same direction as the view. 37 CFR 1.84(p)(1)
   Fig(s) _____
   ____ English alphabet not used. 37 CFR 1.84(p)(2)
   Figs _____
   ____ Numbers, letters and reference characters must be at least
   .32 cm (1/8 inch) in height. 37 CFR 1.84(p)(3)
   Fig(s) _____
13. LEAD LINES. 37 CFR 1.84(q)
   ____ Lead lines cross each other. Fig(s) _____
   ____ Lead lines missing. Fig(s) _____
14. NUMBERING OF SHEETS OF DRAWINGS. 37 CFR 1.84(t)
   ____ Sheets not numbered consecutively, and in Arabic numerals
   beginning with number 1. Sheet(s) _____
15. NUMBERING OF VIEWS. 37 CFR 1.84(u)
   ____ Views not numbered consecutively, and in Arabic numerals,
   beginning with number 1. Fig(s) _____
16. CORRECTIONS. 37 CFR 1.84(w)
   ____ Corrections not made from prior PTO-948
   dated _____
17. DESIGN DRAWINGS. 37 CFR 1.152
   ____ Surface shading shown not appropriate. Fig(s) _____
   ____ Solid black shading not used for color contrast.
   Fig(s) _____

COMMENTS

REVIEWER_____   DATE_____   TELEPHONE NO. _____

ATTACHMENT TO PAPER NO. _____

INFORMATION ON HOW TO EFFECT DRAWING CHANGES

1. Correction of Informalities -- 37 CFR 1.85

New corrected drawings must be filed with the changes incorporated therein. Identifying indicia, if provided, should include the title of the invention, inventor's name, and application number, or docket number (if any) if an application number has not been assigned to the application. If this information is provided, it must be placed on the front of each sheet and centered within the top margin. If corrected drawings are required in a Notice of Allowability (PTOL-37), the new drawings **MUST** be filed within the **THREE MONTH** shortened statutory period set for reply in the Notice of Allowability. Extensions of time may NOT be obtained under the provisions of 37 CFR 1.136(a) or (b) for filing the corrected drawings after the mailing of a Notice of Allowability. The drawings should be filed as a separate paper with a transmittal letter addressed to the Official Draftsperson.

2. Corrections other than Informalities Noted by Draftsperson on form PTO-948.

All changes to the drawings, other than informalities noted by the Draftsperson, **MUST** be made in the same manner as above except that, normally, a highlighted (preferably red ink) sketch of the changes to be incorporated into the new drawings **MUST** be approved by the examiner before the application will be allowed. No changes will be permitted to be made, other than correction of informalities, unless the examiner has approved the proposed changes.

Timing of Corrections

Applicant is required to submit the drawing corrections <u>within the time period set in the attached Office communication</u>. See 37 CFR 1.85(a).

Failure to take corrective action within the set period will result in **ABANDONMENT** of the application.

www.ingramcontent.com/pod-product-compliance
Lightning Source LLC
Chambersburg PA
CBHW080050280326
41934CB00014B/3269